THE
2-HOUR
JOB SEARCH

THE
2-HOUR
JOB SEARCH

Using Technology to Get the Right Job *FASTER*

STEVE DALTON

TEN SPEED PRESS
Berkeley

In loving memory of my mother,
Dorothy Dalton

Library of Congress Cataloging-in-Publication Data
Dalton, Steve, 1976-
    The 2-hour job search : using technology to get the right job faster /
Steve Dalton. — 1st ed.
        p. cm.
    Includes bibliographical references and index.
    Summary: "A job-search manual that gives career seekers a systematic
formula to efficiently and effectively target potential employers and
secure the essential first interview"—Provided by publisher.
    1. Job hunting. 2. Job hunting—Computer network resources. 3. Career
development—Computer network resources. I. Title. II. Title: Two hour
job search.
    HF5382.7.D35 2012
    650.14—dc23

                                    2011036598

ISBN 978-1-60774-170-1
eISBN 978-1-60774-171-8

Printed in the United States of America

Cover design by Katy Brown
Interior design by Chloe Rawlins

10 9 8 7

First Edition

CONTENTS

INTRODUCTION

Technological progress has merely provided us
with more efficient means for going backwards.

—ALDOUS HUXLEY

I've heard numerous theories for why the job search is so difficult
these days: a bad economy, bad luck, outsourcing, cronyism, poor work
ethic, too much reality TV. During my six years as a senior career consultant at Duke University's Fuqua School of Business, I've helped
people of all interests and ages through the job search process, and I
attribute its difficulty to something else entirely—technology.

Technology has made our lives easier in so many ways, but it has
only complicated the modern-day job search. Before Internet job postings grew in popularity in the late 1990s, the job search was a simple
(though tedious) process:

STEP 1 (OPTIONAL). Find classified ads in newspaper.
STEP 2. Mail resume and cover letter to potential employers.
STEP 3. Wait for invitations to interview.

That doesn't sound so bad, right? Ship out resumes and cover
letters, and whoever is interested writes you back. Very straightforward. Of course, those with contacts at the potential employer still
fared best, not having to rely on a piece of paper to make their first
impression for them. But cold calls by phone or mail were often all
it would take to get an interview.

Fast-forward a decade. The Internet's in full swing, websites will find relevant job postings *for* you, and resumes can be submitted online at any hour of the day. Although it's easier than ever before to *find* jobs, why does it now seem so much harder to actually *get* one? In short, technology made applying for jobs so efficient that *hiring* became inefficient.

Throw in a global recession, and suddenly you've got a perfect storm. However, even if the economy were to fully recover tomorrow, the job search still wouldn't go back to how it was.

Technology has effectively ruined the "mail and wait" job search strategy because it is now far more difficult for employers to pick out the few interesting applicants from the massive new influx of casual applicants.

Applying for jobs used to require a significant amount of time. Time to search classified ads in your local paper, type and print your resume and cover letter on nice paper, and package them up in an envelope for mailing. Not everyone had that kind of time, and applying to any job required at least a minimal amount of research— heading to the library to find what address to mail your resume to, for example.

With the Internet, applying for a job can take less than a minute. Google a possible employer's name, click on the Careers section of their website, and submit your resume. Done. When it's that easy, anyone can do it (and everyone does). Thus, recruiters who before Internet job postings used to get a dozen or so applications from mostly local candidates in several weeks for a job now get hundreds or thousands from across the country within hours.

Who has time to read hundreds of resumes? Recruiters today read resumes the way most of us read websites—ignoring a majority of what's on the page and just skimming the headlines—in the case of resumes, usually looking at only schools attended and previous employers, if that.

That's assuming hiring managers actually *look* at resumes received online. My students commonly describe online job postings as "black holes" for resumes, and I agree. Because there is no way for a hiring manager to read all of those applications, the only fair thing to do is not read *any* of them, so online applications may be avoided entirely. (That this attitude saves a hiring manager many hours of additional work is hardly coincidental!) Employers these days rely instead on internal referrals to decide whom to interview. Getting internal referrals efficiently is *the* core challenge of the modern job search, in fact—and we'll return to that topic shortly.

Online job postings are not inherently evil, nor was Becca being lazy by applying for so many jobs online—quite the opposite, actually. She was simply following the same old "mail and wait" paradigm

The Resume Black Hole

I first met Becca (not her real name) in late March, a very high-stress time for MBA students. On-campus recruiting has ended by then, so students without jobs at that point tend to panic. Their May graduation date is looming, and they realize that continuing to avoid the rejection-heavy off-campus search (which most acknowledge they should have been doing all along) is no longer an option.

Like most of her peers, Becca had assumed she would find her job while still on campus—she'd been at the top of her class her whole life, after all. But she hadn't found it, having underestimated the number and caliber of her competitors. She was so anxious that she canceled her spring break trip with a group of her classmates in order to focus on her job search. (Months later, she would call these spring break efforts a "garbage in, garbage out" job search.)

Becca spent her week off scanning job posting websites: Monster, CareerBuilder, Indeed.com, TheLadders, and so on, hoping to find the perfect job. She was frustrated by the fact that all of the marketing positions she found required candidates to have several years of previous marketing experience (which she lacked), but she hoped the strength of her resume—built around her experience at a major accounting firm— would convince potential employers to give her a chance. In one last gasp on her last night of break, she spent *eight consecutive hours* surfing job postings and submitting resumes to dozens of employers.

She never heard back from a single one.

her parents did, except electronically rather than with stamps and envelopes. It *felt* like progress—the websites would say something like "Your application has been successfully submitted," each time (the closest thing she ever got to positive reinforcement in her search), and conventional wisdom said "you reap what you sow" and "hard work pays off." This strategy is also known as "satisficing." "Satisfice" is a hybrid word formed from "satisfy" and "suffice." Coined by Nobel prize–winning social scientist Herbert Simon in 1956, the term describes a person's tendency to select the first available solution that meets a given need, rather than an optimal solution.

Believe it or not, satisficing is actually a good strategy in a majority of cases—it's what prevents us from spending hours deciding which of the dozens of hands soaps to buy at the grocery store. The alternative to satisficing is "maximizing." Maximizing means finding the best possible choice, *regardless of the amount of time or effort it takes*. For major purchases like a home, erring on the side of maximizing rather than satisficing makes good sense, but in most cases satisficing, well, satisfices.

Hiring managers are classic satisficers, which makes total sense. Their ability to make outstanding hiring decisions rarely if ever factors into how big their raise is at the end of the year—therefore, they'll want to spend as little time making hiring decisions as possible. For them, finding a "good enough" candidate quickly is better than finding a "perfect" candidate slowly—so their hiring decision is very unlikely to involve reviewing hundreds of resumes!

The fundamental flaw in Becca's satisficing strategy was that she equated the feeling of making progress with actually making progress. No matter how diligently or efficiently Becca applied conventional wisdom's best practice of pushing resumes and cover letters out to employers through online job postings, she was unlikely to succeed.

Technology in this case had, as Aldous Huxley said, only given job seekers a more efficient means for going backward. It simplified the application process to the point of ruin—the point where its accessibility caused it to no longer help employers efficiently identify qualified candidates. "Mail and wait" simply wasn't designed for the explosion in competition for jobs facilitated by the Internet age.

Technology also gave job search *books* a more efficient means for going backward. It was obvious that technology was changing the job search, so most legacy job search texts introduced "Internet Editions" and "Recession Editions," bolting on more and more advice about incorporating the latest technology fads into the job search without fundamentally revising their "mail and wait" approach. One very well-regarded book even says that networking is the most effective way to find jobs, and resumes are the least effective, but it still spends twice as many pages discussing resumes as it devotes to networking! Inevitably, this has happened:

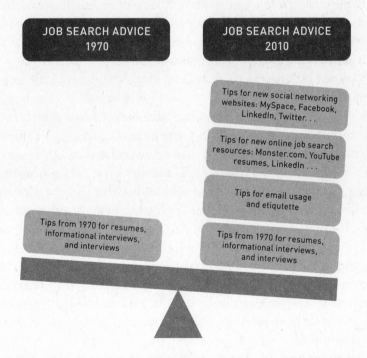

JOB SEARCH ADVICE 1970

JOB SEARCH ADVICE 2010

Tips for new social networking websites: MySpace, Facebook, LinkedIn, Twitter. . .

Tips for new online job search resources: Monster.com, YouTube resumes, LinkedIn . . .

Tips for email usage and etiqutette

Tips from 1970 for resumes, informational interviews, and interviews

Tips from 1970 for resumes, informational interviews, and interviews

But that was just job search books! Job search websites also got into the act, providing article after article revealing the "Top Seven Secrets of the Job Search" or "Ten Quick Ways to Ruin an Interview." In other words, job search advice exploded, and in many cases its goal was to be sensational enough to warrant a click-through, earning attention and/or ad revenue, rather than to actually help people find jobs. Advice was now just as free to publish online as resumes were to distribute, so armchair job search quarterbacks abounded.

Other websites had even less admirable motives—some offered access to "exclusive" job postings if you purchased an upgraded "Gold" membership for a monthly fee, sometimes as much as thirty dollars a month! Every new market offering (even the free ones) had a cost: energy.

In his book *The Paradox of Choice*, psychologist Barry Schwartz discusses a study in which participants were allowed to select a free Godiva chocolate—some were allowed to choose from a box of six, and the others from a box of thirty. The surprising finding was that those who chose from the box of six actually were *happier* with their decision than those who had more to choose from. This can be attributed to a concept called *decision anxiety*.

When picking from a box of six chocolates, making the right choice is relatively easy—you either like nuts or you don't, you prefer dark chocolate to milk or white, and so on. However, in a box of thirty, you have only one-in-thirty odds of making the optimal choice. You may be tempted to examine each chocolate before making your choice, losing time as well. You may even feel stressed after eating your chocolate, when you wonder whether you should have chosen differently. (Meanwhile, our caveman brain is simply thinking, "Chocolate taste GOOD!")

Similarly, a job seeker has to take time—sometimes just seconds, and other times minutes or hours—to decide which articles to read and which websites to subscribe to. This taxes both our speed and our willpower. A growing body of evidence supports the fact that focus (or more precisely "executive function") is a finite resource that is drained every time we are tempted—even in an entirely unrelated venture. A 1998 Case Western Reserve University study found that test subjects who were told to eat only from a bowl of turnips despite the presence of a nearby plate of warm chocolate-chip cookies gave up on a subsequent challenging task more quickly than those who were told they could eat both the turnips *and* the cookies.[1]

Welcome to the modern job search.

It's OK if this is all stuff you are hearing for the first time. Historically, career centers have always taken a "maximizing" approach toward career education—teaching students everything they should theoretically do during a job search, regardless of the time each step requires. Career centers have never really taught the job search in terms of energy preservation, which is more important now in this age of information overload than it ever was before.

I myself was blindsided by how poorly equipped I was for the modern job search. A few months into my post-MBA marketing job I'd spent my whole life targeting, my boss pulled me aside and presciently told me, "Steve, this may not be the right career for you." I was *reeling*.

After the shock and denial wore off, I saw she was spot-on in her assessment. The job routinely minimized my strengths and accentuated my weaknesses, frustrating me so thoroughly that I dreaded the sound of my own alarm clock every morning. So I decided to look online for a process on how to get organized for conducting my very first post-graduation "off-campus" job search. However, click after click, all I could find were laundry lists of general advice, rather than a coherent process. Even worse, the laundry lists tended to be *long*, and their advice tended to be terrible. Here are some of my favorites:

- "Have a powerful resume."

  Thanks, coach.

- "Go to local career fairs."

  Really?

- "Use your contacts."

  You're not helping.

- "Start a blog."

  Right after I finish making that video resume . . .

- "Take people's job search suggestions with a grain of salt. Be selective and apply the advice that works best for you."

So few words, so much irony.

The reason I hated such careless advice then (and now) is because—although it was delivered in optimistic and inspirational tones—it gave no consideration whatsoever to the limited amount of spare time I actually had. As Barry Schwartz himself said in *The Paradox of Choice*, when we are given too many choices, "Choice no longer liberates. It debilitates. It might even be said to tyrannize." Even while unemployed I wouldn't have the time to trial-and-error my way through all of that advice, and even if *somehow* I did, following tips like "Wear a T-shirt that says 'Please Hire Me' into an interview" (true story) would save me the worry of *ever* being employed again.

That said, there is no way around the fact that the only way to get internal referrals is through networking. That doesn't mean you have to *like* networking to get a job. Liking it is totally optional, but it *is* necessary. Personally, I hate networking. I am terrible with names and worse with faces, and I had no idea how to leave a good impression with new people I met. You know how some people bring the party with them? Well, I bring the awkward with me. However, I simply *had* to find a way to compensate for this limitation. I wanted instructions for doing that, not advice—I couldn't find it, however. Therefore, that is what I will bring to you in this book.

For the lucky minority out there who feel no anxiety at all when someone mentions networking, if you're thinking that makes this entire book irrelevant, please think again. In today's job search, networking without an underlying strategy is just as ineffective as mailing-and-waiting.

Vivek (see sidebar, page 9) was correct in identifying the importance of creating personal relationships with recruiters, but he didn't use the technology available to him to diversify his efforts or manage his follow-up effectively, smothering those he sought to impress. Technologies like job search engines and social networking websites have unlocked a totally new, highly efficient way to job search, but

The Low-Tech, Low-Tact Approach

Another student I worked with, whom I will call Vivek, had (unfortunately) come to my attention before we had even met—he had made waves among both his classmates and his recruiters for his pushiness.

Vivek wanted to become a strategy consultant with (and only with) an elite firm, and he was incredibly focused in his efforts. He would attend every event this handful of firms sponsored, meet every representative the companies sent, and unfailingly send them thank-you notes the next day. So far, so good. Regrettably, although his networking skills in the moment were (mostly) correct, his overall strategy was not. Vivek was so desperate to leave a positive impression that he ended up talking more than he listened, veering away from genuine relationship building and toward a transparently transactional and quantity-based networking approach—a common mistake among those who focus on too small a universe of firms.

One of my MBA classmates—now a recruiter for one of those elite firms—called me a couple of weeks after one of their events to catch up, and before hanging up he gingerly asked me, "By the way, do you know Vivek?" Uh-oh.

Apparently, my former classmate had remembered Vivek monopolizing his time at their event, and he winced when he saw an informational interview request from him less than a week later. (For the uninitiated, informational interviews are conversations that sympathetic contacts will grant to answer job seekers' questions and/or prescreen them for an actual interview.)

Just as my classmate feared he would, Vivek used that informational interview to ask tedious questions very similar to those he had asked in person just a week before. This oversight could have been forgivable had Vivek not requested similar conversations *on the very same day* with several other recruiters from that event as well.

As expected, Vivek did not get an offer from his handful of top-choice firms—they found him well qualified but overzealous, making them uncomfortable at the thought of putting him in front of clients. Vivek was devastated and spent. All of his job search efforts stopped for nearly a month as he mentally recovered from watching his entire strategy collapse.

it requires forgetting some of what you've learned before. "Mail and wait" as a strategy is obsolete, and a strategy that relies only on low-tech networking is equally off the mark.

The name of the game in today's job search is a mix of high- and low-tech—specifically, using technology to locate a living, breathing advocate for you within your target employers as efficiently as possible. *That* is what this book will help you do. *Networking* is simply another way to say "acquire internal referrals"—and adding that little bit of specificity to a vague task makes it far easier to address systematically.

The 2-Hour Job Search works because it applies the Pareto principle to the job search, focusing on only what you need to know, rather than on all of the things you could possibly know. The Pareto principle, more commonly known as the 80-20 Rule, states that in most situations 80 percent of the results can be attributed to 20 percent of the actions taken. It is named for Italian economist Vilfredo Pareto, who noted in 1906 that 80 percent of Italy's land was owned by 20 percent of its population (and that 80 percent of his own garden's peas came from 20 percent of his peapod plants, though that may just be urban legend). Interesting, but how does that concept get put to practical use?

In the business world, it can be used to prioritize efforts. In 2002, Microsoft CEO Steve Ballmer acknowledged that 80 percent of crashes in Windows and Office were due to only 20 percent of the programs' bugs.[2] The programmers could have spread their time equally among all known issues in a quest for perfection. Alternatively, they could have addressed the easiest errors first to show quick results. However, both of these strategies would have had less impact than their chosen path, which was to focus on the most disruptive 20 percent of issues first. Some of the less disruptive issues were likely *never* solved (surprising no Apple fans whatsoever), because new versions of each software package were soon released, rendering the remaining repairs unnecessary.

The job search is no different. There are immeasurable opportunities to be distracted by unnecessary details, and it takes discipline to stay focused. Most of my students are so busy that they have only a couple of hours a week to devote to their search, so for them—as for anyone seeking a job while employed or a parent, for example— achieving a high degree of efficiency is essential. *The 2-Hour Job Search* provides that discipline by teaching readers a formal job search process that ensures they benefit from the 80-20 Rule at every step. It's not only for new MBAs, either; it works just as well for younger job seekers like law school graduates and newly minted undergrads in humanities or engineering as it does for experienced professionals looking to change jobs mid-career.

What I propose in this book could not have been done even ten years ago—neither the technology nor the information was readily available, and what was available would have taken weeks or months to track down rather than just two hours. Older readers will remember hours spent in front of card catalogs and towering bookshelves at their local library to research a paper that today's students can now research entirely from home (and at any hour!). Because technology now allows for better target identification and relationship building, it should certainly be used.

In its simplest form, the job search of today requires three distinct steps—*Prioritize, Contact,* and *Recruit*—and each step gets its own in-depth treatment in this book. Prioritization is essential before embarking on a job search; otherwise, the infinite information available online becomes overwhelming and impossible to navigate. Once targets have been identified, you need to initiate Contact before you can secure any advocacy. Once a sympathetic contact is listening, you can Recruit that individual to become your advocate.

The titular two hours refers to the amount of time it takes to achieve liftoff, which in this book means to complete the first two steps: Prioritize and Contact. After that, your job search effectively goes on autopilot during the Recruit step. Further effort will be required, but it will become nearly automatic in nature—you'll know exactly what to do when.

Lastly, it's important to note that this book is *not* a comprehensive job search guide. Such a book would be quite lengthy and mostly unnecessary—much like buying a travel guide to all of South

America when you plan to visit only Peru. Here's a summary of the major steps of the job search process, and where this book fits in:

Choose what you want to do

Write a resume

} **THE**
2-HOUR
JOB SEARCH

Prioritize target employers

Contact target employers

Recruit advocates to provide internal referrals

Interview

Select an offer

There are several popular references readily available for tactical information on choosing a career, writing a resume, and honing your interviewing skills—frankly, these processes have not changed much for quite a while, so the need for a new approach there is not as urgent as one for landing that first interview. This book focuses only on the topics for which to date there has been *no* widely accepted process or set of best practices. In other words, *The 2-Hour Job Search* starts you at the point after you identify what you want to do, and it ends once you secure formal interviews with your target employers, at which point existing resources are once again helpful.

Also note that there is technology that I will *not* discuss in this book—for example, tracking RSS feeds in Google Reader. There is no shortage of interesting technology out there, but that doesn't mean it's all useful and/or necessary. This book wasn't written to teach you about all of the many job search resources available to you. *The 2-Hour Job Search* strives more for "right-tech" than "high-tech"— truth be told, the latest isn't always the greatest. This book's mission isn't to impress you with all that technology *can* do—its mission is to help you harness well-established (and free!) technology to make this process as pain-free, efficient, and effective as possible. In short, this book details the exact job search process I would follow myself, knowing what I know now.

I now teach this process to every new Duke MBA student during their first few weeks on campus. Although I enjoy helping students improve their resumes and interviewing skills, I consider my work developing and sharing the 2-Hour Job Search to be a moral obligation. An on-campus job search is a luxury students enjoy only temporarily—the vast majority of one's job searches are experienced as alumni, far away from a university's friendly confines. Although this book is helpful for on-campus job searches, it is critical for post-campus ones.

After many iterations of teaching this material, I've found that my audiences frequently ask the same questions in a similar order each time. Therefore, I'll follow a similarly ordered question-and-answer format to help you follow along and digest the material. At the end of each chapter, I'll feature a Troubleshooting section covering a few of the most commonly encountered challenges, along with instructions for navigating each.

In terms of what you'll need on your end to follow my process, please make sure you have access to the following:

- Spreadsheet software, like Microsoft Excel or iWork Numbers
- An email program with an integrated calendar, like Microsoft Outlook, Apple Mail, or Google's free Gmail and Calendar applications
- A LinkedIn profile (see *LinkedIn Start-Up* sidebar, page 14)

I'm happy to say that both Becca and Vivek's stories have happy endings. After working with me to learn and execute his own 2-Hour Job Search, Vivek secured an internship with a boutique consulting firm, and Becca received a full-time brand manager offer from a Midwestern food company. Becca's story didn't quite end there, however—through her 2-Hour Job Search investigations she came to realize that she found human resource management more appealing than pure marketing, so she declined her brand management offer. I asked her whether she wanted to meet me for help with restarting her search, and she told me, "Thank you, but I know what I'm doing now!" That comment made me smile for weeks.

LinkedIn Start-Up

LinkedIn is a (free) professional social networking site, and it proves very useful at various points in the 2-Hour Job Search. If you don't already have a LinkedIn profile, create a basic one now by registering at LinkedIn.com and supplying basic information about your prior/current employers and education. You can do this in five to ten minutes—filling out your profile more completely with descriptions of each position held can take several hours, but that is not critical to this process and therefore you can skip it until after you've gotten underway with your search.

To fully benefit from LinkedIn's capabilities, you must invite people to join your network. To get started, search for your favorite (and/or most popular) coworker, boss, friend, and family member, and invite each of them to connect to you. This will give LinkedIn's technology an idea for who else is likely in your social network, and it will suggest people you may also want to connect to from there.

In addition, once your initial contacts accept, their networks will be notified that you've joined LinkedIn, so others will start reaching out to *you*. Thus, with no further effort of your own, your online network will build in the background. This won't give you a complete online network immediately, but it will give you a great foundation for when we more actively engage LinkedIn in chapter 5.

In addition, LinkedIn allows users to join Groups, which also allow you access to larger networks of people. Some Groups allow you immediate membership; others will need to verify your status before allowing you to join, so it's good to initiate those processes before you need them. Search Groups for previous schools and employers, and join any groups that apply to you.

Similarly, find relevant Groups related to general interests, like clean energy or the Atlanta metro area, for example. Sharing a group with a potential contact allows you greater visibility into his or her profile when a match is found, so this is another way to quickly expand your network on start-up.

PRIORITIZE:
The LAMP Method

## CHAPTER 1

LIST

What is LAMP?

The LAMP Method (List, Alumni, Motivation, Posting) is a systematic, efficient seventy-minute process for making a prioritized list of target employers (although no individual action takes longer than fifteen minutes to complete, making it easy to start and stop as time permits). The critical goal in this section is to end up with a list that is *precisely* ordered based on a set of criteria predictive of job search success. The ordering precision is important so that you know exactly which target employers to focus on first, second, third, and so on.

Why make a list?

In 2008 there were 27.5 million businesses in the United States, and 99.9 percent of those had fewer than five hundred employees.[1] Furthermore, a full 99 percent had fewer than one hundred employees! Take a look for yourself:

	2008	
EMPLOYER SIZE (#)	ESTABLISHMENTS	JOBS
Total	23,947,096	165,870,794
Self-employed (1)	36.1 percent	7.0 percent
Stage 1 (2–9)	55.7 percent	32.3 percent
Stage 2 (10–99)	7.7 percent	34.9 percent
Stage 3 (100–499)	0.4 percent	14.2 percent
Stage 4 (500+)	0.05 percent	11.6 percent

The Stage 3 and 4 companies may be the first ones that come to mind, but they make up less than 0.5 percent of the total population of employers available, and between them they account for only one-quarter of all employment in the States.

That means that unless you are willing to target only less than one-half of a percent of the total number of employers out there, there are far more targets than one has time to consider. (Two-thirds of all U.S. jobs are at employers with between two and ninety-nine employees!) The vast majority of those smaller employers don't have the presence or the budget to travel far and wide looking for the best talent available—and the larger firms don't usually need to try too hard to find applicants. In most cases, they will be quite happy with "good enough" talent who are proactive and make it easy for the employer to hire them.

Because there are now databases that allow job seekers to find these twenty-four million employers, it is more important than ever to identify a subset that are of particular interest before you begin, so as to avoid being overwhelmed by the possibilities out there. Before the Internet, geography and limited information organically managed this boiling-down of possibilities quite well, but those times are no more.

By creating a list of employers, we are essentially drawing the borders of our job search; this makes filling in the relevant hiring details of those employers a finite and minimally stressful activity, just like coloring in the pictures in a coloring book.

A good example of how making a list of target employers is effective can be found in an unlikely source: reality television. On ABC's *The Bachelor*, twenty-five women are isolated in a house and given a chance to form a relationship with one eligible bachelor. Based on the Bachelor's whims, one or more women are eliminated each episode until only one winner remains. Voilà. Romance.

Watching this show physically pains me—I have a very low tolerance for awkwardness, which for a career coach is like being a doctor with a latex allergy—but I've always found its game theory fascinating. Who *wouldn't* be a good Bachelor if you limited supply and maximized demand like that? I mean, the guy has a 100-percent chance of winning; his entire strategy consists of "Get my own TV show."

On the flip side, being a female contestant on *The Bachelor* is an awful proposition. Supply is artificially restricted and demand is artificially inflated. Each woman has just one-in-twenty-five odds of winning, and she also forgoes a month or so of normal dating activity (and perhaps a job as well) in order to play—and she hasn't even *seen* the guy! It's dehumanizing and a long shot at best, so who would do such a thing?

Sadly, every year I see dozens of very smart people do exactly this—voluntarily subject themselves to situations with high competition and low odds of success (online job postings, most commonly), desperately hitching their hopes to one bachelor at a time until someone gives them a chance. There are numerous downsides to this approach, but the worst of all is the toll it takes on one's confidence. I have seen men and women who've lived their whole lives at the top of their class be shaken by the job search to the point where they will accept *anything* just to make the anxiety stop. The better job searchers may seriously pursue three to five opportunities at one time, but if none pan out they too must start over again from scratch.

The bachelorette's fate in the reality show game ultimately rests in the hands of the Bachelor, much as a job seeker's fate rests in the hands of the hiring manager of the moment. In game theory terms, a bachelorette could employ two methods to improve her chance of "winning": increase the odds of the game (say, finding a dating show on which only ten women compete rather than twenty-five), or increase the number of times the game can be played. An even better approach, however, is to adopt the mindset of the Bachelor himself: collect a large number of preliminary candidates, narrow them down by collecting key pieces of information about each one, and focus primarily on the strongest ones. That is effectively what the LAMP Method does for job seekers—it changes them from one of many bachelorettes into the Bachelor himself.

Why make a LAMP list, specifically?

The LAMP Method allows for efficient gathering of specific, useful employer information, providing black-and-white data for choosing which employers to approach and in what order.

LAMP guarantees efficiency in two main ways: it ensures that similar tasks are grouped together and that each task is done to the appropriate level of detail—and no further. It accomplishes this by limiting research to three easy-to-access pieces of data that in my experience have proven to be most predictive of job search success: Alumni, Motivation, and Postings. These factors are proxies for more important pieces of information, and they will later be used to prioritize your target employers so you approach the most important and time-sensitive ones first. In short, LAMP uses the 80-20 Rule to get 80 percent of employer research's benefit in 20 percent of the time. Heeding the words of Voltaire, we will not allow the perfect to be the enemy of the good.

In this chapter we're going to discuss how to create a robust List (the L in LAMP) of potential target employers, and in the subsequent chapters in this section we will examine how to quickly find information about Alumni, Motivation, and Postings. At that point our LAMP list will be completely filled in, but we will need to properly sort it to complete the Prioritize step of the two-hour process. Thus, Step 1 of this book (and the time required to complete the task covered in each chapter) looks like this:

	TIME REQUIRED
Chapter 1: Compile **L**ist of possible employers	40 minutes
Chapter 2: Identify **A**lumni	10 minutes
Chapter 3: Assess **M**otivation	5 minutes
Chapter 4: Classify **P**ostings	15 minutes
Total for Step 1	70 minutes

There will be great temptation during the LAMP process to cheat and fast-track an interesting target employer, but if you give in, in that moment you've lost your efficiency. Rest assured that following LAMP's steps correctly will get you back to any intriguing opportunities within two hours.

How long should my target employer list be?

Forty employers.

Can I start with fewer than forty employers?

You could, but the effectiveness of the 2-Hour Job Search drops dramatically if you do. It is an attrition-based job search strategy, meaning that most of the employers that you start the process with will be eliminated along the way. In the LAMP stage, employers are eliminated (or, more accurately, de-prioritized) because they are of lower interest and/or do not offer positive indicators of employment. Starting with fewer than forty employers results in a weaker target employer list that usually skews toward high-profile organizations that tend to draw a lot of competition for open spots, resulting in a longer, more difficult job search and less leverage when a match is found.

Should I exceed forty employers, then?

Absolutely, if you can do so within the time limits provided. The more possible employers, the better. It costs little additional time to add possible employers at this point of the process, just as it takes little time to send a few additional units through an assembly line when it's already up and running. Exception-handling is what takes most of your time. Thus, if you find a resource that with minimal effort can give you twenty more potential employers when you're already sitting on thirty, copy in all twenty—do not artificially end your list at number forty!

Some of the job seekers I've worked with say this step alone was the most helpful aspect of the 2-Hour Job Search. To reinforce its importance, let's do a quick thought experiment. Picture in your mind an ice-cold bottle of soda pop—what brand is it? Now think of another brand. And another brand. And lastly two more.

Did Coke and Pepsi make your list? When presented with an open-ended question with many possible answers, people tend to select items with the highest name recognition. Job seekers often adopt the same approach, sometimes putting little more effort into their target companies than those that first come to mind. Deciding on whom to approach for employment is stressful, so it is perhaps even rational behavior to minimize the time spent performing it—however, it is counterproductive in the long term. If everyone followed this strategy, nobody would ever work for lesser-known companies— and even Microsoft was one of those back in the 1970s!

One year I offered new Duke MBA students a rich incentive to create a LAMP list of target employers—namely, the right to have first pick of their second-year mentors, ensuring that their mentor would have the most relevant experience to the new MBA's upcoming search. Now, most students could immediately think of five to ten employers for whom they wanted to work. These are not enough targets to ensure success, however, especially because so many students' picks were likely to overlap if they targeted the same function (like investment banking or consulting). Students who don't expand their consideration set beyond the usual suspects often fail to find a job with any of them. In that case, a period of depression and a suspension of effort lasting weeks or even months often occurs before the job seeker can muster the energy to start over again.

Employers are *very* effective at determining which candidates do and do not have other options if their organization doesn't extend them an offer; some will even ask directly which other employers you've been speaking to. A lot of it is simply a matter of confidence—employers like seeing it, and people with options (be they job seekers or reality-show Bachelors) demonstrate it more than those without.

Some of my students showed me lists of twenty possible employers before slinking into my office and swearing there were absolutely no other employers out there to consider. However, a twenty-employer list doesn't go far enough to force creativity and help people find the right job. The best careers (and easiest job searches) are rarely found through 100-percent rational or linear thought. In my experience, those who find the job search process least stressful are the ones who combine their aptitudes with their personal passions. Why is that? Two main reasons.

1. They genuinely enjoy learning about the employers to whom they speak, rather than seeing such conversations as just a means to an end. One of my most motivated job-seeking students, Adam, had been an IT consultant before business school, and he desperately wanted to break into the mobile phone industry despite not having a relevant background. He just adored following the industry. He hit the pavement and truly enjoyed talking to the contacts he made at the major firms, but none had any jobs for him. Still, his efforts paid off. How?

2. They experience less competition when they target nonobvious employers. For Adam, a contact at the fourth mobile phone company he spoke to recommended he talk to a colleague of his at the organization that sets standards across all mobile phone manufacturers to ensure compatibility. He did so, and the first question they asked him was "What do you know about the mobile phone industry?" Bingo.

Because of his prior conversations using the 2-Hour Job Search's process for informational interviewing, Adam was easily able to discuss the major trends impacting the industry, the challenges the current market leaders were facing, and where he thought the new technology was headed. They offered him a job the next day. When you have knowledge, people want to hire you. When you have both passion and knowledge, people want to hire you *immediately*.

That is not to say that personal passions can or must be the centerpiece of every job you ever have. In fact, some postpone a more enjoyable career to accomplish other personal or professional goals first—working for a while as an investment banker is a great way to earn seed money for your future start-up company or career in a nonprofit organization, for example.

However, when it comes to the length of a target employer list, I want to make sure my students have applied some creativity and considered their next step if their present top-targeted career is not "the one." Compelling them to complete a list of forty possible employers accomplishes this nearly every time. I've seen this simple act liberate students mentally to the point where they admit their initial career search focus—those first five to ten employers—was more of a family or peer expectation than a personal passion, and they decided to shift their job search focus ahead to that "future" career immediately. Powerful stuff.

A more unconscious process takes over when job seekers are pushed beyond the obvious choices. What websites do they check for ideas? What magazines do they flip through to get inspired, and which articles catch their attention? How do they spend their weekends, for that matter? Those personal default inclinations and interests are really where exceptional and fulfilling careers lie. Optimal career selection is not the main focus of this book, but it is one further benefit in addition to increased job search efficiency and reduced stress.

Finally, a large target list encourages job seekers to consider smaller employers. As we learned earlier, 99.9 percent of employers have fewer than five hundred employees, yet that other 0.1 percent of employers tends to capture our attention most of the time, making us feel (with the help of often massive advertising budgets) that they are the only options available. They certainly are not, so you should *not* rule out employers with whom you are simply unfamiliar during this list-making exercise.

A bachelorette from *The Bachelor* could dramatically increase her odds of finding a mate by dating in non-TV venues because she could then be considered on her own merits instead of vis-à-vis twenty-four competitors. Similarly, lesser-known employers will attract less competition, increasing the odds that you will be considered on your own merits instead of on your qualifications relative to hundreds of other applicants.

Most of those employers you're unfamiliar with will likely never need to be researched further in the 2-Hour Job Search because they won't display any positive indicators of likely job search success. However, some will give you a compelling reason to research them later—perhaps through an alumni connection or open job posting, for example. It costs very little time to include additional employers (both well known and unknown) early in the process, but trying to add them later is very time-consuming.

So how do I do this within forty minutes?

There is an old proverb that asks "How does a man eat an elephant?" The answer is "One bite at a time," which has always struck me as very wise. Anything is possible—even a seemingly overwhelming situation—if you develop the ability to break the project into small, manageable pieces.

LAMP users may generate their forty-employer list in an infinite number of ways, but in my experience four approaches have proved most efficient: (1) dream employers, (2) alumni employers, (3) posting search, and (4) trend-following. I ask my job seekers for "ten employers or ten minutes," whichever comes first, for each one:

METHOD	BENEFITS	BEST FOR JOB SEEKERS WHO ARE . . .
Dream employers	Research is applicable to multiple employers	• Targeting a specific industry
Alumni employers	Have contacts at every target employer	• Targeting a specific role/job title • Restricted by geography • Undecided about their career • Shy
Posting search	Target employers are currently hiring	• Targeting a specific role or job title • Restricted by geography
Trend-following	Learn about industry while researching; locate less-obvious employers	• Switching careers • Seeking smaller employers

As a reminder, not all employers your research uncovers will be well known, but you should include any that match your search criteria in your LAMP list at this point in the process. Those that are neither familiar to you nor offer hope for employment are quickly screened out later.

APPROACH #1: DREAM EMPLOYERS

The "dream employers" approach consists of first adding the employers you have always aspired to work for in your spreadsheet's "L" column and then systematically looking up each employer's peers and adding them into your spreadsheet as well. This approach works best for readers targeting a particular industry, because any research done on one company will likely apply to their competitors as well.

Database services often charge fees for usage, so if you do not have free access to them via a university or public library, skip these services and use the surprisingly useful free options like Wikipedia and Google. Let's assume for example that your first dream job is to do graphic design for a sports company like Nike. That company's Wikipedia page provides links to relevant product categories like "athletic shoes." And that page provides a list of nearly twenty major athletic shoe brands and a link to a separate page with a more comprehensive list of more than one hundred shoe makers! For a graphic designer interested in working for a sports apparel company, his or her company list could be generated in under five minutes by copying and pasting this list into the L column of the LAMP spreadsheet.

If you do have access to the subscription-based databases, my job seekers tend to like Hoovers, OneSource, and DataMonitor360 best—each provides its own unique competitor lists for most dream organizations, and any competitor can be selected to reveal the competitor's competitors as well. (These services also allow for easy creation of company lists by location, industry, size, and many other criteria.) For example, looking up Kraft's competitors in any one of these databases or free search resources like Yahoo! Finance may reveal the following list of companies, all of which might appeal to a geographically flexible candidate:

ConAgra Foods, Inc.	Omaha, Nebraska
General Mills, Inc.	Minneapolis, Minnesota
H.J. Heinz Company	Pittsburgh, Pennsylvania
Kellogg Company	Battle Creek, Michigan
PepsiCo, Inc.	Purchase, New York
The Coca-Cola Company	Atlanta, Georgia

Sara Lee Corp.	Downers Grove, Illinois
The Hershey Company	Hershey, Pennsylvania
The Procter & Gamble Company	Cincinnati, Ohio
Frito-Lay	Dallas, Texas

No single list from any source will be more or less correct than the others. Both free and paid search resources can offer you a great list of employers to start from quickly, especially if you are interested in working for large companies.

The reason the dream employer approach works so efficiently is its use of the 80-20 Rule—the competitor lists are not comprehensive or perfectly relevant, but they are easy to access quickly, and those employers you rule out later still help put you in the mindset of the Bachelor rather than one of many bachelorettes.

You may be *very* tempted to research unfamiliar companies as you go, but resist that urge. Your progress will slow dramatically if tasks are blended—you will move from a simple copy-and-paste operation requiring little thought to a complicated operation with multiple, simultaneous goals and scores of small decisions. "Should I click on that link? Should I read this block of text?" Each decision and sidetrack may take only a few seconds and minimal effort, but both the time and the mental exertion add up quickly.

If the temptation to click around is too great, at least cap your efficiency losses by committing to the One-Click Rule—if you can get the information you want within one click, go for it. However, if that click does not provide sufficient information, the possible employer gets added to your list and you move on. Remember, one major benefit of LAMP is that it helps you identify less-obvious employers and systematically determine which of them to investigate further based on whether they offer any positive employment indicators. So multiple-click research on employers that *will* be targets is efficient; multiple-click research on employers that only *might* be targets is not.

The goal is ten possible employers in ten minutes, leaving a job seeker interested in food and beverage marketing with a LAMP list that looks like this so far:

#	LIST	ALUMNI	MOTIVATION	POSTING
1	ConAgra			
2	General Mills			
3	Heinz			
4	Kellogg			
5	Pepsi			
6	Coca-Cola			
7	Sara Lee			
8	Hershey			
9	Procter & Gamble			
10	Frito-Lay			

A law student's LAMP list may look like this after the first ten minutes of effort:

#	LIST	ALUMNI	MOTIVATION	POSTING
1	Cravath, Swaine & Moore			
2	Skadden, Arps, Slate, Meagher & Flom			
3	Womble, Carlyle, Sandridge & Rice			
4	Jones Day			

#	LIST	ALUMNI	MOTIVATION	POSTING
5	Hunton & Williams			
6	Kirkland & Ellis			
7	Sidley & Austin			
8	White & Case			
9	Wyrick, Robbins, Yates & Ponton			
10	Tharrington Smith			

I encourage you to find more employers in that span of time, but if you come up with fewer than ten, don't spin your wheels and try to force it. Just move on to the next method.

Oh, and just like that, you earn your first check mark!

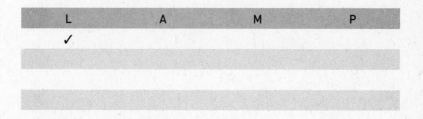

L	A	M	P
✓			

One down, three to go.

APPROACH #2: ALUMNI EMPLOYERS

The "alumni employer" approach consists of accessing your most recent college or university's alumni website and searching through the organizations employing other graduates of your program for ideas. This approach works very well for those targeting a specific city or state. Just enter your geographic constraints (for example, "San Francisco") into your most recent alumni database, and if any alum has an interesting employer or job title, copy the employer's name into your list and move on.

This strategy is also effective for those uncertain of what career they would like to pursue next, because any open-ended search (for example, by location, or in the media and entertainment industry) will generate a list of alumni with very different job titles at a wide assortment of organizations. Some jobs will seem more appealing than others, and identifying a few job titles you'd like to fill will greatly simplify your search, both in the alumni database and elsewhere. Just as with the previous location-based search, copy any employer that looks interesting into your LAMP list and keep going.

Finally, if you're shy about approaching strangers, this approach is ideal because you'll locate only employers for whom you'll have at least one alumni contact.

As a final reminder to stay true to the LAMP process, it is important to not copy and paste alumni contact information during this procedure. It may seem efficient to capture that data at this time, but that's exactly wrong for two main reasons. First, capturing that data now involves switching applications—for example, from your web browser to your spreadsheet and back—many, many times. Each time takes thirty seconds or so when you factor in the copying and pasting, and each shift in focus is a potential opportunity for distraction.

Tip: Set *All* Search Results to "Show All"

In any database, be sure to maximize the number of results shown on any one screen. Changing Google's default setting for search results per screen from ten up to one hundred reduces the number of clicks needed to review all results by up to 90 percent. In *Superfreakonomics*, authors Steven Levitt and Stephen Dubner highlight a study that says "cognitive drift" sets in any time a computer user must wait more than a second after a mouse is clicked for the screen to change, so each click represents an opportunity for distraction if a website is slow to load.

Change this setting in all alumni databases and job posting websites you frequent to similarly improve your speed while getting a better overview of available information.

Second, you'll only ever need alumni contact data for a fraction of your possible target employers (and even then only for one or two alums at each), so gathering all alumni contacts at all forty targets involves a lot of unnecessary work.

A singular focus is what makes each LAMP step so fast, and in this step you are simply listing possible employers. That said, skip a line in your spreadsheet to differentiate the employers found using each of the four approaches—it will save time later.

And with that you get your second check mark.

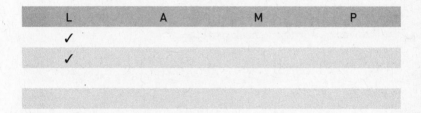

L	A	M	P
✓			
✓			

APPROACH #3: POSTING SEARCH

The "posting search" approach consists of selecting possible employers from the list generated by a job search engine (I find Indeed.com to be most comprehensive). Job search engines differ from employment websites like Monster.com by searching all employment websites, as well as all corporate websites (like BestBuy.com), simultaneously in one search.

The key advantage to this approach is that it limits results to just those companies that are hiring now. It also enjoys one of the same benefits as the alumni employer approach in that it easily performs searches that are restricted to a specific geography or function (for example, marketing or computer programming). It's also very easy to use—Indeed.com specifically asks for only two inputs: "what" and "where." In "what" you'll input keywords (like your most recent degree, if relevant) or job titles of interest (like "chemical engineer" or "graphic designer"). In "where" you'll enter specific cities, zip codes, or states of interest, if desired. After that, click "Find Jobs" or press Enter, and within seconds you have a list of actively hiring employers you can add to your LAMP list.

However, the posting search approach also presents a LAMP user's biggest risk of inefficiency. It can be awfully tempting to click on interesting-looking postings for more info, rather than just copying and pasting the employers' names into your LAMP list per the instructions. This is akin to taking an impromptu break on moving day to look through old photo albums or yearbooks—a complete momentum-wrecker. Again, trust that proper LAMP technique will return you to these interesting postings within two hours, with a solid strategy and peace of mind.

Now add your third check mark.

L	A	M	P
✓			
✓			
✓			

"Intern" Beware

The 2-Hour Job Search is identical for an internship search except for one modification—internship seekers should be careful about using the word "intern" in their search terms during the posting search approach. Far fewer internships than full-time positions are posted online—in general, adding the word "intern" to your search terms on job search engines like Indeed.com will reduce the quantity of your results by a factor of one hundred.

That does not mean the word "intern" should not be a part of the search—it definitely should! However, when you find that too few results are being returned, "intern" is the first word you should delete. Even if an organization is not recruiting interns, the fact that they're recruiting full-time employees suggests they are in good enough financial shape to add further personnel, temporary or otherwise.

APPROACH #4: TREND-FOLLOWING

By now, your list should have around thirty possible employers—ten from each of the three previous methods. "Trend-following"—that is, finding "trending" employers—is the last of the four strategies you will try. Very simply, in this ten-minute period, I want you to Google the industry or function of your choice (for example, solar energy or engineering) along with the word "trends." A number of articles will appear, and given the simplicity of your search terms, they are likely to be macro level, which is perfect for someone trying to learn more about a new industry.

Spend these ten minutes skimming some of these articles to see what shifts are occurring in your targeted market, but more important, keep an eye out for any organizations mentioned in these articles for doing new and interesting things. This method not only informs but also identifies smaller organizations that are looking to get their name out. Attracting qualified talent may be an expensive proposition for these organizations, so talent that approaches them, driven by a genuine interest in their line of business, will enjoy a significant advantage. Job seekers I've worked with who have used this method have in some cases advanced immediately to a final-round interview, simply through the initiative they showed in finding that employer in the first place. Regardless, the trend-following approach gives job seekers critical information about which sectors are hiring, where and how the market is changing, and which organizations are best positioned to take advantage of those market shifts.

Now you're ready to highlight the L column in your spreadsheet and sort alphabetically. This will help you screen out duplicate entries. That is the end of the L task. Forty minutes or forty employers later, your LAMP list should look something like the example on page 34 (which we will further develop and reference for the remainder of the book):

#	LIST	ALUMNI	MOTIVATION	POSTING
1	Ace Tomato Co.			
2	BiffCo			
3	Darlington Electronics			
4	Hanso Corporation			
5	Initech			
...	...			
...	...			
...	...			
39	Staypuft Marshmallow Inc.			
40	Zamunda Airlines			

By eating the job search elephant one ten-minute bite at a time, you have completed a list of forty employers in forty minutes.

L	A	M	P
✓			
✓			
✓			
✓			

And with that, we can bid the L step adieu.

L	A	M	P
✓			

TROUBLESHOOTING

What if I don't recognize an employer—should I include them in my list?

Absolutely. It takes only a moment to include them at this point in the process, but it takes far longer to add them later. Only a subset of employers with which you are unfamiliar will ever need to be researched, and those will become readily apparent near the end of the LAMP Method.

Realize that demand for employment at most employers is proportional to their brand awareness; the smaller and less well known an employer is, the less competition there is likely to be for employment there. Therefore, including on your LAMP list some less-obvious employers that are close to your interests is an effective hedge.

What if I am an international citizen seeking to work in the United States, but I lack permanent U.S. work authorization, which some of my target employers require?

The process is still essentially the same, but because you will need your future employer to sponsor a U.S. work visa (usually an H-1B visa), you should populate your LAMP list as much as possible from organizations found in the U.S. Department of Labor's annual list of employers who sponsored such visas last year. (Online vendors offer more user-friendly versions of this same list—I personally use GoingGlobal's H-1B Plus tool; if you are a current student, ask your career center about this resource. If not, myvisajobs.com offers a database with similar search capability for free as of this writing.)

The theory behind this strategy is that an organization that sponsored an H-1B visa last year is more likely to sponsor another one this year than an organization that did not.

That said, the smaller the organization and the better your previous experience fits a target employer's needs, the less critical it is that they appear on the Department of Labor's list. Large well-known multinationals will get top-caliber talent even if they restrict applicants to

continued

U.S. candidates only, because demand for employment at those firms is usually high. They are incentivized to exclude international candidates for two main reasons: cost and expansion. Visa sponsorship for international candidates costs several thousand dollars per hire, between visa and lawyer costs, so large employers with human resources departments that can afford to cut this cost without compromising their new hires' talent level will do so. In addition, most multinationals' expansion is coming from outside the States right now, so their preference is to employ foreign students studying in the States back in their home countries, where they have market expertise and can be paid the local market wage (which is usually lower than a U.S. wage, presenting those carrying U.S.-based education debt with a difficult conundrum).

Smaller employers are less likely to have formal rules about the work authorization requirements of potential hires—they may simply want to hire the best candidate possible, regardless of his or her background. Remember, hiring managers are more interested in finding "good enough" talent quickly than "perfect" talent slowly, so if you are an otherwise superior talent to what they'd find in a U.S.-only talent pool, and you find them instead of vice versa, you may be surprised how willing they are to work with you.

The best way to use these online databases is to rule out large employers who don't appear, but rule in small employers who do. Using these databases to exclude small employers who don't appear is counterproductive; this may simply mean that the employer did not hire *anyone* last year (or that the few hires they did make just happened to be domestic candidates), which would prevent their appearance in such databases. However, those small employers who *do* appear to have sponsored a work visa for jobs of interest to you should definitely be included in your list!

Regardless, it is incumbent upon you to educate yourself on your visa requirements and/or consult an immigration attorney to learn how to best explain your sponsorship situation to potential employers. Most immigration attorneys will provide such advice for free in the hopes you'll later choose their firm to actually do your paperwork filing for you, so don't be shy about asking!

What if I can't list any dream companies because I don't know what I want to do?

The first step is to *relax*. Very few people know what they want to do. A vast majority of my MBA students—whose ages typically range from the late twenties to early thirties—go to business school specifically so they can change careers! I've worked with alumni in their forties and fifties about making similar changes, and it all boils down to the same common challenge—finding a way to combine your strengths with your passions.

Of the two, your strengths are probably the easier to assess. What have been your proudest moments in life professionally up to this point? Why were they so, and what unique skill or blend of skills was required to pull it off? Here's a more engaging way to consider this question: If your life depended on naming a skill at which you think you're in the top 1 percent of the world, what would it be? (This is a *very hard* question for most people, by the way—but it often is inflammatory enough to get my clients thinking in the right direction!)

Assessing passions can be more difficult. If you don't have time to read books on self-assessment, pick up the latest issue of the *New York Times* or *Bloomberg Businessweek* and mark the articles you're most interested in reading. Don't actually read them—simply flag them and keep looking. After you've found a few that have caught your eye, determine what those articles have in common. Once you've done that, you may well be on the way to figuring out what you want to do with your life.

I believe that people can be mediocre at anything they really set their mind to, but you'll only be great (and happy)

continued

at jobs you're passionate about—industries or markets where it's easy to soak up information because you care. When you find a subject for which information jumps into rather than out of your head, you're on the right track, and starting with that topic where you think you're in the top 1 percent of the world is a great strategy.

What if my search criteria yield too many results (more than one thousand)?

Adjust your threshold for how interesting you need an organization to be before you'll include it in your list. For example, if your Posting method search terms are "MBA" and "marketing" and you get one thousand results, you would need to copy one out of every one hundred organizations, on average, into your spreadsheet to reach ten using the Posting method. However, being too careful about picking organizations increases the chances that you may time out and exceed your ten-minute time frame, so at around five hundred to one thousand hits or more, it is better to try to add some additional descriptive words to your search to limit your results. Also, remember to change your Indeed.com preferences to show fifty postings at a time rather than the default ten postings. Fewer clicks mean a faster search and fewer distractions.

What if my search criteria yield too few results (fewer than twenty)?

This can be challenging at first, as selecting only well-known organizations typically will result in a list of five to ten possibilities at most. A major additional benefit of starting with forty potential employers is that it requires job seekers to probe a bit deeper into the relative importance of certain constraints applied to their search. For example, is it more important to get a job in finance or in North Carolina? That an employer is well known or is in the high-tech sector?

TROUBLESHOOTING

When the most important aspects of your next job are clarified in this way, new potential employers are introduced into the process. These less obvious options tend to be better matches, feature less competition, and offer better compensation for any open positions that are available than the big fish who can rely on their name recognition to attract a lot of interest.

What if this takes longer than forty minutes?

In nearly all cases where this step takes longer than forty minutes, the LAMP followers are researching unfamiliar organizations as they go or are perusing interesting-looking job postings instead of copying down the employer's name and moving on. Remember, this entire process can be completed within just two hours if done correctly, so following the process properly will get you back to that interesting posting within two hours at most.

Each time you switch between tasks (for example, from employer-copying to researching postings), your rhythm breaks and speed diminishes. Worse still, this break in concentration increases the probability of distraction via cognitive drift (see page 30). If you find this step in the process progressing slowly, this is the likely culprit.

If not, the other main reason for slow progress is being too precise in choosing which organizations to add to the list, which usually occurs when you are unwilling to include unfamiliar organizations to your list per the instructions. These hidden gems are where a job seeker can go from being one of twenty-five bachelorettes to being the Bachelor, because few candidates will have the skill and desire to both discover and contact that outfit. It may not be your dream employer, but it will be a good job search insurance policy and a great source for relevant information if you are also pursuing larger organizations in the same industry. In general, if you find yourself debating whether or not to include an organization you find on your list, it's faster just to include it than to debate whether or not to include it!

## CHAPTER 2

ALUMNI

Why are alumni so important? Isn't the 2-Hour Job Search about using technology?

It *is* counterintuitive—one might assume technology would make alumni (and their relatives, "connections," and "contacts") unnecessary in the modern job search, but in fact they are more important now than ever before.

I had always heard that alumni are an important part of the job search, but for most of my life I never really understood why. When I was an undergrad in the late nineties, the economy was dot-com strong. Many companies were coming on campus to interview, so it really did feel like there were enough jobs for everyone. Alumni to me were just nice old men and women who'd show up at social events, completely detached from the world of recruiting.

Fast-forward to my years at business school in the early 2000s. The dot-com bubble had burst, and the economy had slowed dramatically. On-campus jobs were still available, but there was much more competition for them. The companies provided only a limited number of interview spots, and the alumni who attended those recruiting events in the weeks leading up to interviews decided who got them.

Gone were the days where I could just show up to an interview and hope to wow them there; now I had to earn my audience. I went from totally disregarding connections to obsessing over them. I had heard countless times that I should "use my network" in the job search, but I had never learned *how* to actually do so.

Being qualified on paper used to be sufficient (or at least a great advantage) in the job search—now it is inadequate by itself. A qualified candidate still requires *internal advocacy* in an organization to raise his or her credentials above the noise of the many other casually submitted resumes that online job postings have made possible. The 2-Hour Job Search was developed to create this important network of internal advocates quickly and effectively.

I must clarify one important point at this time—when I use the term *alumni* in this book, I am referring not just to literal alumni (fellow graduates of the schools you've attended). I am referring to any contact who is sympathetic to your cause and may advocate for your eventual recruitment. Literal alumni are *usually* the most easily accessible source of potential internal referrals, so we'll focus on them exclusively in this chapter to approximate the level of preexisting advocacy available at your target organizations. Once we complete our LAMP lists, I will teach you (in Step 2: Contact) how to use more advanced technologies and techniques to fill in gaps for employers where no literal alumni are available. However, because these tactics take additional time, we'll use them only with top-priority employers for whom we have no simpler options.

Before we go ahead and fill in our A column, though, I have some good news—you have completed the hardest part of this process! The 2-Hour Job Search from here on is like a highly effective autopilot—it takes over during the tedious but necessary job search steps (like looking up alumni at target employers, for example) so you can conserve your time and energy for the steps that are more sophisticated and engaging (like gaining the trust and advocacy of those alumni you've located).

If filling in your L column felt like an art, the remainder of your LAMP list is science. So get ready to make a lot of progress quickly.

Making West Virginia Eat Healthier

Chip and Dan Heath, in their excellent book *Switch*, confront how to create change when change is hard.

One critical element of invoking change, according to their book, is "scripting the critical moves," or providing specific, actionable instructions for accomplishing a goal. The Heath brothers told the story of two health researchers in West Virginia who identified the dire need for state residents to adopt a healthier diet. However, instructing West Virginians to "eat healthier" was unlikely to produce any real results. They had to think of a more specific way to create a change in diet.

The researchers themselves adopted the 80-20 Rule, and they saw that whole milk happened to be very popular, especially in rural communities. However, it is also the single largest source of saturated fat (the bad kind) in the average American's diet. Thus they chose to focus there, because a majority of Americans drink milk.

Piloting their concept in two communities, they ran radio and TV ads encouraging residents not to vaguely "eat healthier," but specifically to buy 1-percent milk instead of whole milk at the grocery store, illustrating the point in their ads through gimmicks like equating the amount of saturated fat in a glass of whole milk to *five* strips of bacon, or bringing to their press conferences a tube full of the same amount of saturated fat as a gallon of whole milk. They also cleverly noted that families will drink whatever is in the refrigerator, so they recognized that the key was to change the purchasing behavior of West Virginians— their consumption behavior would naturally follow.

This specific approach was effective. In the pilot communities, the market share of low-fat milk shot up from 18 percent before the campaign to 41 percent immediately after, and it held at 35 percent six months later. By providing clear direction, a difficult change was achieved.

Consider the 2-Hour Job Search to be the path for fundamentally changing the way you approach the job search. While you are following this book's explicit instructions for executing an effective search, millions of other job seekers will be struggling to put advice like "use your network" to practical use (the job search equivalent of being told to "eat healthier"), giving you a significant advantage.

Remember, you are the Bachelor in this process—not one of hundreds of bachelorettes! Winning is inevitable—it just takes the right infrastructure (this book) and a little bit of time.

How do I look up alumni for forty employers in ten minutes?

The answer is simple: focus. Henry Ford's Model T made automobiles affordable for the masses for the first time, and the secret to its success was the same: focus.

Cars used to be a luxury for only the rich when they were introduced in the late 1800s. Their cost was necessitated largely by the heavy labor costs associated with their by-hand assembly. Ford launched the Model T in 1908 with the vision that it would be the middle class's first car due to its low price, simple design, and quality materials. The concept took off, and soon Ford was having trouble keeping up with demand.

One of Ford's employees, William "Pa" Klann, saw a potential opportunity for manufacturing improvement while visiting a Chicago slaughterhouse. Klann watched as cow carcasses were placed on conveyor belts that ran past various cutting stations. At each station, a butcher would remove the same cut of meat, over and over and over. This minimized the amount of expertise any one butcher needed and maximized their efficiency by bringing their work to them rather than requiring them to physically switch between stations or mentally switch between tasks.[1]

Klann thought this "disassembly line" process used in reverse would allow for cars to be built more cheaply and efficiently. Klann took this assembly line concept to his superiors, where it eventually caught the attention of Henry Ford, who decided to implement it for the Model T in 1913.

With the assembly line's introduction, production time for the popular automobile plummeted by nearly 90 percent, from 12.5 to 1.5 hours per car.[2] Ford also needed fewer workers to operate the assembly line, and those workers required far less training than their predecessors. This labor savings allowed Ford to make Model Ts even more affordable to consumers. When the Model T was introduced, it sold for $850. By comparison, most other cars at that time were selling for $2,000 to $3,000. After the assembly line was implemented, in 1916 Ford was able to reduce the Model T's price even further, to $360—the equivalent of about $8,000 today. Ford's own line employees could now afford one on just four months' pay. By eschewing the concept of "multitasking" decades before that term existed, Henry Ford effectively "put America on wheels."[3]

The key takeaway from this story is that reducing a complex process (making a car or looking for a job, for example) to individual simple tasks increases efficiency and reduces the mental effort required. Focusing on a repetitive task may certainly be boring, but it gets tedious tasks completed quickly, effectively, and with minimal stress.

For our A column, all that is required is a singularity of focus and an alumni database. Let's return our attention to our example LAMP list from page 34.

Now, log in to your most recent college or university alumni database. Most, if not all, accredited undergraduate and graduate institutions have this technology available now, and usually there is a link to the alumni directory shown prominently on your school's alumni website. If you don't know your login ID and password, call your alumni office—you're going to need it!

Although you can likely search alumni by name, location, and many other criteria, right now we are interested in just the employer search field. One by one, search each of your LAMP list employers to see whether each has one or more alumni currently employed there. Enter "Y" in your Alumni column if yes and "N" if no.

The temptation here is to copy and paste the alumni information you find, or even worse, to copy, paste, *and format* that information to fit your spreadsheet. This is wasted effort, even though it may seem efficient to capture it while you're there. In reality, for most of these companies you will never need more alumni information than the "Y" or "N," and for those you do, you may need it for just one person. It is far faster to go back into the alumni database after your top ten employers are identified than it is to copy and paste it for forty or more potential targets up front. The 80-20 Rule is still in effect here.

Just like a good hiring manager, we are not looking for perfect information about our targets slowly—we are looking for "good enough" information quickly—so that Y or N will do just fine for now.

With that introduction, log in and populate the "A" column. Yes, it's tedious, but pour yourself a glass of your favorite beverage and you'll be done before you know it, leaving you with something that looks like this:

#	LIST	ALUMNI	MOTIVATION	POSTING
1	Ace Tomato Co.	Y		
2	BiffCo	Y		
3	Darlington Electronics	N		
4	Hanso Corporation	Y		
5	Initech	N		
...	...	...		
...	...	...		
...	...	...		
39	Staypuft Marshmallow Inc.	N		
40	Zamunda Airlines	Y		

And with that . . .

L	A	M	P
✓	✓		

We can now move on to the third part of our LAMP list—we're halfway there!

What if my graduate school is small with few alumni?

If your desired career is closer to your graduate degree than your undergraduate degree, start with your graduate school's alumni database anyway. Yes, there may be fewer alumni in the program for you to locate, but they are more likely to be at relevant employers. In general, the smaller the alumni database, the more helpful the alumni.

What if my undergraduate school is small (as well)?

There is no minimum acceptable number of alumni you need to have for your list—some lists I've seen have fewer than 5 to 10 percent Ys in the Alumni column. For right now, we just want to get a sense for how big and relevant our preexisting network is.

Later in this process, once we identify your top-priority employers, we will expand the definition of "alumni" to include those with whom you share a personal or common-interest connection rather than an academic one. These bonds can be just as powerful as alumni connections, if not more so, but they do take more time to locate, which is why we reserve them (at least initially) for only top-priority employers without alumni.

What if I have been out of school for many years?

In this case, you may wish to substitute a LinkedIn People search of first-degree, second-degree, and Group connections in lieu of literal alumni connections in your first pass.

LinkedIn is a social networking website geared toward professional rather than personal information-sharing. Just like Facebook, once you join, you will connect with your friends and colleagues through an invitation process. Also like Facebook, you will be able to join groups and view your friend's contacts. However, where LinkedIn outdistances Facebook for job search purposes is its ease of use for finding contacts at target employers and telling you who your "closest" connection is to those people.

A first-degree connection is someone in your immediate network whom you've connected to via invitation, whereas a second-degree connection is someone who shares a mutual connection with you. A group connection is someone who has joined one of the same affinity groups on LinkedIn that you have. All three of these groups of people will be your next-richest source for "alumni" if you do not find applicable contacts in your alumni database(s). You will learn more specifically in chapter 5 about the "strength of weak ties," or the disproportionate usefulness of acquaintances' social networks (as opposed to your close friends' or family's) in relation to your own, but keep building your immediate LinkedIn network in the meantime. The more colleagues you're connected to on LinkedIn, the higher your likelihood of finding a relevant second-degree contact at a high-priority target employer will be.

That said, if speed is of the utmost importance, or you are in a field related to your most recent graduate degree, you should still start with your most recent alumni database, because those contacts will be more immediately relevant and more quickly accessible than those for whom you require an intermediary's assistance.

Does the same go for Facebook? Should I start building my network there as well?

Absolutely. It won't be as directly applicable to your job search as LinkedIn, given its social rather than professional focus and its inability to highlight degrees of separation, but its "status update" option will prove useful for top-priority employers where alumni databases and LinkedIn prove unhelpful. We'll discuss this further in chapter 5 as well.

continued

TROUBLESHOOTING

I used my graduate school's alumni database to complete my Alumni list. Should I now check my undergraduate school's alumni database for any employers I marked as Ns?

No. If you have a graduate degree, there is no need to search your undergraduate school's database right now. Similarly, if you started with LinkedIn, there is no need to repeat the process for previous alumni databases. We'll go back and do this on an as-needed basis. The idea is to move through this process quickly, getting 80 percent of the information we need in 20 percent of the time, and leaving any detailed work for later, if we recognize that it is necessary.

What if this step takes longer than ten minutes?

The most common reason for this running longer is either trying to capture additional alumni information—like names, locations, and so on instead of just "Y" or "N"— or checking multiple alumni databases instead of just your most recent one. Checking only your most recent alumni database will suffice for your purposes right now.

What if very few of my target employers have alumni?

In this case, it is all the more important that you determine which few actually do, because those alumni may be your best conduits to other knowledgeable people in the industry whom you can enlist to advocate for you. However, now is not the time to worry about how that part gets done. We will cover that in Steps 2 and 3 later. Remember—one step at a time!

## CHAPTER 3

MOTIVATION

I already know Motivation is important, so can I skip this chapter?

Of course you *can*, but I wouldn't. It's both the most important *and* the most overlooked step of the process—a devastating combination. Plus, it literally takes only five minutes. This section will take you longer to read than it will to execute, but doing both will save you a lot of time down the road, because this will be the most important criterion we sort our list by once it is completed.

What is so important about Motivation?

Motivation is the engine that ultimately drives your job search forward. Thus it is *the single most important* factor when ranking your targets. Even if I give you perfect instructions for conducting a job search, without your willingness to execute those instructions, success is impossible.

Too often I see job seekers spend valuable time pursuing employers they are not interested in for one of two main reasons: (1) the application is easy, or (2) they happen to be inspired during a random moment to "get something done." Certainly, it's important to strike when the iron is hot, motivation-wise. However, following inspiration randomly throws job seekers grievously off-course, because "sunk costs" rather than genuine preferences begin to drive the focus of future efforts.

What are sunk costs, and what do they have to do with the job search?

Sunk costs are expenses (not just of money, but also of time and effort) that cannot be recovered. Let's say I buy a ticket to see the latest Michael Bay movie, and I realize about an hour in that it's *terrible*. Like, truly truly awful. Offensive not just to me but to my ancestors as well. I may be tempted to stay for the remainder of the movie because I paid good money to watch this insult to filmmaking. However, the ticket price is a sunk cost—I can't get that money back, so I'm out ten dollars regardless of whether I stay or go. Similarly, I can't ever get back the hour of my life that I've already invested in this travesty. That time is also a sunk cost.

One might argue that because I'm that far into the movie, I might as well finish it—I paid for it, after all, and I'm already halfway to the end. This is the risk of sunk costs—you start making decisions based on previous decisions you regret rather than on rational criteria. The rational action, in economic terms, is to disregard sunk costs—my ten-dollar ticket and hour of time already invested—and go do something else of higher entertainment value. Housework, for example.

In the job search, without a prioritized target list, you can start unintentionally prioritizing poor targets at the expense of richer ones. This can happen for any number of reasons. Let's say you just applied to Company X, which you find underwhelming as an employer, but perhaps your friend knew the hiring manager there or you saw a job posting online and just got inspired in that moment to "make it happen." At this point, your future decision making is susceptible to corruption by sunk costs.

Your rational brain thinks, "If I spent time applying to Company X, then I should also spend equal time applying to every employer I like more than Company X." Depending on how little you liked Company X, this can result in an impossibly large to-do list!

This enormity may scare off some job seekers entirely, just to avoid facing the natural shame one feels after making a mistake. However, an even worse scenario is *actually applying* to every employer you like better than Company X, simply to rationalize that previous Company X application. Unfortunately, such a shotgun approach does not allow time for the degree of follow-up necessary to succeed with any employer in today's market.

In Vegas they call this "throwing good money after bad," or investing more money into an already bad investment. Guilt, rather than rational thought, is driving one's actions in this case. The right approach—both in Vegas and in the job search after pursuing a mediocre employer—is to walk away. The time invested in Company X is a sunk cost—it can't be recovered. However, this is much easier said than done.

Walking away from a bad investment requires nerve, and as we learned earlier, such decisions tax our limited supply of executive function. Once we apply to a proverbial Company X, the internal debate about whether to commit to that shotgun approach or walk away can, in itself, wear a job seeker out, resulting in the true worst-case scenario: exhaustion without anything to show for it.

So how do I avoid becoming a victim of sunk costs?

Don't do *anything* randomly in the job search. There is nothing random in this book—we've already decided which employers are in our initial consideration set (otherwise known as everything in our L column), and we will let the data we are in the process of collecting dictate the order in which we will pursue them.

In this step, we will leverage a concept called "arbitrary coherence" to quickly yet accurately categorize our level of interest in each potential target. This step couldn't be simpler. It takes only five minutes and requires no research (it *forbids* it, in fact!), but it is perhaps the most ignored step of the job search among those I encounter, even though it saves job seekers hours of headaches, confusion, and anxiety later.

What is arbitrary coherence? Why does it enable this step to go so quickly?

In his classic text *Psychometric Theory*, the late Vanderbilt professor Jum Nunnally wrote:

> *Whereas people are* notoriously inaccurate *in judging the absolute magnitudes of stimuli, e.g., the length of a line in inches, they are notoriously accurate in making comparative judgments.*

In short, we compare well, but we measure poorly. For example, imagine I show you a brand-new lawnmower, and I ask you to rate its appeal on a scale from 1 to 10, with 10 being highest.

Most of you won't have previous experience rating lawnmowers, so your answer will be meaningless to me without further explanation. Basically, if you score it a "5," I won't know what "5" means. You may have been playing it safe with the scale provided, because you have no idea whether you'll like future lawnmowers better or worse. Conversely, you may have *hated* the lawnmower, but would never rate anything you couldn't make yourself lower than a 5. I simply don't know.

Once I ask you to rate a second and third lawnmower, however, your ratings will start to make sense relative to one another. I still won't know what a 5 means, but I know with a high degree of certainty that you like the 5 a little bit less than a 6, and much less than a 9 or 10.

Arbitrary coherence is a concept that says that, although an initial rating of one in a series of items is largely arbitrary (and can be highly influenced by random suggestions), subsequent ratings will be coherent with respect to the first one.[1] In other words, the relative ratings will be correct, even if the absolute values are useless.

Most novice job seekers tend to begin with a too-small universe of possible target employers. When I see a target list with only a handful of employers on it, I have no idea whether those employers are truly that job seeker's favorite targets or were simply the first employers that came to mind or showed up in a basic job posting search. I'm regularly shocked by how little thought job seekers give to identifying potential targets—"convenience" is the most common driving force, so when pursuing the employer ceases to be convenient (which it always does), many job seekers lose their desire to continue pursuit.

In this book, we will employ some job search jiu-jitsu to use arbitrary coherence—our susceptibility to largely arbitrary initial opinions—to our advantage. We'll declare an arbitrary anchor—in this case, we'll classify our favorite target employer as a 5—and rate all our employers relative to that one on a scale of 0 to 5.

How does this step actually work, then?

In this step, we'll vertically work our way down the Motivation column in our example from page 34, filling in Motivation scores one by one for each of our targets.

Starting with the first employer in our LAMP list, rate your level of motivation to pursue each one on a scale of 1 to 5, *using only the information you know about each employer right now*. No outside research is allowed (I'll explain why in a moment).

Remember, your favorite employers are 5s, so second-tier choices are 4s, third-tier choices are 3s, and least-preferred employers will receive 2s. We'll reserve 1s for target employers we don't know anything about. Those 1s will serve as placeholders for later, after we sort our list. However, *under no circumstances* should you research these targets right now—not even to find out what they do or where they're located!

Why not?

It's very inefficient. You've introduced a second goal into what was a straightforward single-goal process. It's impossible to research and rank employers at the same time; what you'd really be doing is switching back and forth between researching and ranking. Every switch requires two mental steps: "goal-shifting" and "rule activation."

When you write email while watching TV, you're shifting goals (from working to entertainment) and activating new rules (from grammar and syntax to listening comprehension) dozens of times per hour.[2] Viewed as a two-part process, multitasking suddenly seems pretty complicated.

Researching facts is the polar opposite of providing general opinions, so the risk here of losing your place is higher than you might think. Keep this simple task simple, relying on only your current personal opinions, and in five minutes you'll have a beautiful, completely filled-in M column that looks something like this:

#	LIST	ALUMNI	MOTIVATION	POSTING
1	Ace Tomato Co.	Y	4	
2	BiffCo	Y	5	
3	Darlington Electronics	N	4	
4	Hanso Corporation	Y	3	
5	Initech	N	1	
...	...	...	...	
...	...	...	...	
...	...	...	...	
39	Staypuft Marshmallow Inc.	N	5	
40	Zamunda Airlines	Y	1	

In my book, that earns you another check mark:

L	A	M	P
✓	✓	✓	

We're just a fifteen-minute step away from finishing our LAMP list and learning which employers are worth our time and which need to go find themselves a different Bachelor!

TROUBLESHOOTING

What if relocating to (or remaining in) a certain area is essential to my search, but I don't know where many of my LAMP list's employers are located?

In those cases, temporarily disregard location in your Motivation rating for that employer. Pretend it's neither good nor bad—just a total nonissue—and award it your preferred Motivation score. Then, for employers whose location you do not know, take the Motivation score and subtract 0.5 points from it, leaving you with a score of 4.5 for a dream employer, for example. (Make sure your spreadsheet is set to show you one decimal place, in this case—you don't want to see your 4.5 automatically turn into a 5 because of formatting.)

Once we sort our list, we'll see whether any employers with motivation scores ending in a 0.5 are close to the top of our list, and we'll research those all at once to quickly determine their location. At that point we can change our Motivation score up or down accordingly.

What if I don't use any or many 2s (or any other number) in my M column? Is that OK?

This is totally fine. Most of my students don't use many 2s, either, because most employers they knew well enough to give 2s to were screened out before they were included in the L column.

continued

TROUBLESHOOTING

The 2 rating—if used at all—tends to show up most often when a list of employers meeting certain criteria during the L step was copied and pasted into the L column wholesale. That's actually a very good approach, because giving an employer a 2 rating here, after importing it as part of a list, accomplishes the same objective much more quickly than doing separate copy-and-pastes to winnow out employers from your list in the first place!

What if a majority of my ratings are 1s, because I'm not familiar with the employers in this industry/region?

That is just fine, and a great illustration of how LAMP saves you time. Before LAMP, you may have felt pressured to research all of those employers individually, which likely would require hours of effort. Using LAMP, we'll leave them all as 1s for now, and once our list is complete, we'll see whether any of those 1s give us a reason to believe they could be a compelling employer, through either an alumni connection or a current job posting.

Those employers will be worth researching ASAP, whereas the other 1s can postpone learning about until we get down that far on the list (if at all).

CHAPTER 4

POSTING

 15 MINUTES

Didn't we already use job postings in the L column of our LAMP list?

Yes, we did, but in this final part of Step 1, we're going to use a job search engine to fill in an entirely separate Posting column. In this column we will rate the quality and quantity of job postings an employer currently has available. Those with better postings are more time-sensitive (and therefore higher-priority) targets; thus, they will get a higher score in your P column, just as you gave higher Motivation scores to the employers you found more interesting in our last step.

But didn't you compare job postings to "black holes" earlier?

Yes, I did. It's a bit contradictory—that something could both be helpful and a waste of time—but let me explain.

Online job postings (and the job search engines that find them for you) are helpful in several ways, but they are *terrible* at actually getting you a job. Their real value is the meta-information they provide.

What is meta-information?

The Oxford English Dictionary defines the prefix "meta" as "self-referential," so meta-information is information about information itself.

I have two good friends from business school, Hank and Katie. Hank is a true savant—he knows everything. He's therefore a mainstay on my Wednesday night trivia team at Bull McCabe's Irish Pub here in Durham, North Carolina. Katie, on the other hand, doesn't know everything in the same way Hank does, but she can *find* information extraordinarily well. If you can think it, she can find it. Need a current article about the cotton candy market in Canada? No problem. Want a scholarly paper identifying the best aromatherapy scents for curing a toothache? She's on it.

In other words, Hank has a gift for *information*, whereas Katie has a gift for *meta*-information. The good news for Katie is that meta-information is a greater asset in today's job search than information itself.

Before online job postings flourished, finding out which employers were hiring was the main challenge. Now it's easy to find out who's hiring—it's just impossible to get their attention. Knowing who the hiring manager is is helpful information, but it is a one-off luxury rather than a strategy. Knowing how to systematically *find* the hiring manager is meta-information, and it's crucial in the modern job search.

So if online job postings aren't good for getting you a job, what *are* they good for?

Job postings—more specifically, job search engines like Indeed.com—provide great information about what sorts of jobs are available in a particular city, as you learned during the L step earlier. However, for the P step, we're more interested in job search engines' ability to tell us who's actively hiring *right now* versus who is not.

It would have been hard to explain earlier, but the data we've collected in each of these last three steps—Alumni, Motivation, and

Postings—are themselves meta-information. They're proxies for more important information—facts that would be prohibitively difficult or time-consuming to determine precisely, so we're using a quick 80-20 Rule approach instead.

What are the A, M, and P columns proxy information *for*, then?

Your Alumni column is a proxy for the likelihood of finding a sympathetic contact at that employer. You'll never know perfectly just from someone's name whether he or she would be willing to help you, but those you share an academic (or other) background with are more likely to help you than those who don't.

Your Motivation column is a proxy for your willingness to actually do the work necessary to get that job. This was hinted at in the last chapter. Regardless of how strong your network is at an employer, landing an offer takes work (like writing thank-you notes and conducting informational interviews). If you're genuinely fired up about that employer, you're far more likely to put in that work. Connections can get you in the door, but passion and follow-through are what get you the job.

This Posting column is a proxy for urgency. We know that as soon as employers post a job they become overwhelmed by applicants, so if one of your top targets has posted a job, you must find an advocate there ASAP. Postponing your outreach to those firms for a week or two may take you out of the running.

As I mentioned earlier, Motivation is the most important criterion for sorting our employers; current job postings are second. Thus in this step we're going to categorize the current hiring activity of each target in terms of time sensitivity. This categorization will help us choose which employers within a particular Motivation level (all of your 5s, for example) we will approach first.

Alumni do indeed come in third out of three for our eventual target sorting, but that has less to do with their relative importance and more to do with our ability to find substitute sympathetic contacts when literal alumni are not available. This conversion process takes time, however, so we use it only when absolutely necessary. We'll cover this topic further in the next chapter. First things first; let's finish off our last column so we can sort our list and see who our top targets are!

How do I fill in the P column, then?

The P column will take about fifteen minutes for a forty-employer list—longer lists will take more time, but only marginally so. However, the temptation to cheat here will be significant—you will return to Indeed.com (featured earlier in our L step) to search for postings, but you *must not* click on any interesting ones you find—use only the search results themselves (that is, job titles) to make your decisions! Trust me: if you do this step correctly, you'll be back to the good job postings within thirty minutes, but if you do it incorrectly, it will take *hours*—if not entire days.

I have tested several different job search engines head to head, and as of this book's printing, Indeed.com has consistently been the most comprehensive in terms of the postings it finds. The Indeed.com interface consists only of entry fields for "what" and "where." In this step we're only concerned with "what." However, unlike the way we used Indeed.com in the L step—starting with keywords, job titles, and locations—this time we're going to start with the employer names from our LAMP list to see what hiring they are doing right now.

This will be an 80-20 search, though—we're looking for good information quickly, rather than perfect information slowly. Done right, this step takes only fifteen minutes, but that involves adopting a policy of "strategic ignorance"—in other words, you'll need to willingly ignore interesting information.

Rather than actually clicking on and then reading the (inevitably lengthy) postings that a job search engine points us to, we're able to approximate an employer's hiring activity based on the search results themselves! A job title, a web address, and a few snippets of text are totally sufficient. Then we move on to the next employer on our list.

Just as in the Alumni step, the details aren't important right now—we can go back for those later. The high-level information is what we're after—in this case, "Are they hiring right now?" and "If so, is it for positions I'm interested in?"

Not coincidentally, filling in our Posting column is going to be very similar to filling in our Alumni column. We'll start with the employer at the top of the list and systematically work our way down, rating each employer as we go.

However, whereas a Yes or No answer sufficed for the Alumni column—either you found an alum at each employer or you didn't—using a Yes/No answer for the Posting column may result in important information getting lost.

Finding relevant job postings for each target employer is the best-case scenario. However, sometimes you'll find less relevant job postings, such as positions in a different department or at a higher level. This gives you the important meta-information that the employer is doing *some* hiring rather than none—it's not under a total hiring freeze. That's a better signal of potential employment than no postings at all. Thus, as a default, rate Postings on a 3-point scale from 1 (for no postings whatsoever) to 3 (for relevant postings).

To get this step done quickly, we need to operate systematically. Thus we'll search each employer for an ideal posting—if we find one, the employer gets a score of 3. If we don't, we'll search again for *any* postings. If we find any, the employer gets a score of 2; if not, it gets a 1. Then we move to the next employer. Lather, rinse, repeat.

To search for an ideal posting, we will first enter the employer's name into the Indeed.com "what" field, followed by a probable keyword about the job we're seeking, such as "manager" for a retail manager or "designer" for graphic designers. For example, let's assume we're seeking a graphic design position. The first employer in the sample LAMP list we're developing is "Ace Tomato Co.," so our "what" field should look like this when we press Enter:

"Ace Tomato" designer	SEARCH

Tip: Use Quotes in Search Fields

Surround an employer's name in quotes if it contains two or more words. If we don't—for example, if we search for General Electric instead of "General Electric"—any relevant search results will be overwhelmed by many unrelated ones.

If Indeed.com finds any matching job postings, it will list the following information for each:

- Job title
- The posting's website address
- A couple of lines of text from the posting that include our keywords

This information alone is sufficient for us to determine Ace Tomato's Posting score. This is an essential point, so allow me to say it once more with feeling:

UNDER NO CIRCUMSTANCES SHOULD YOU CLICK THROUGH ON THESE JOB POSTINGS! Massive danger lies ahead here if you click through; doing so will obliterate your time, efficiency, and energy—guaranteed.

Job seekers' overwhelming temptation upon finding an ideal posting is to drop everything and race to complete the online application. Remember, though, that submitting a resume online is meaningless without an internal advocate and a lot of follow-up effort. (There is truly no benefit to being 1st, let alone 300th, in a pile of resumes nobody will ever look at!)

Therefore, it is better to hold off on initiating contact with your targets until you know which ones are top priorities. This course of action may even make the online application entirely unnecessary— if, for example, you find the right contact or decide the target is not a priority—saving you even more time. All that matters for us right now is "Is this employer a 1, 2, or 3?"

Back to our example—if we get zero results from our "'Ace Tomato' designer" search, we know we won't give Ace Tomato a Posting score of 3 right now. The next step is to repeat the search with just the company name (deleting the job-specific keyword "designer") to see how actively Ace Tomato is hiring overall:

"Ace Tomato"	SEARCH

If we get back any postings here, we'll give Ace Tomato a Posting score of 2 for "some hiring activity." However, if we get zero results once again, we can safely assume Ace Tomato has no online job postings available, and we'd give it a Posting score of 1.

Granted, Ace Tomato may actually *have* openings—job search engines aren't perfect, and not all jobs get posted online. However, the important fact is that their openings are not easy to find—for us or anyone else! Thus this opportunity is less time-sensitive relative to our other targets that *are* recruiting online.

If we do in fact find some postings for Ace Tomato, searching only on the company's name, here's how we evaluate which Posting score the company receives. We will quickly peruse the *job titles only* to see if any seem relevant—sometimes our targets may call our ideal jobs by different names. For our example, some firms may call their graphic designers "graphic artists" or something similar, meaning they *are* actually hiring graphic designers right now, just with a different name. If that is the case, we'd give Ace Tomato a score of 3, even though it didn't actually contain the word "designer."

Tip: Maximize Search Results

Change the Indeed.com settings so it shows the maximum number of results per page—this allows you to skim job titles most quickly for the info you need.

However, if after a quick skim we don't see any relevant job titles in the postings, we'd give Ace Tomato a Posting score of 2. They are hiring—just not for anything we're interested in. Thus they are less important to contact quickly than our 3s, but more so than our 1s (our targets with no postings whatsoever).

After entering the correct Posting score for Ace Tomato, we'll click Back on our web browser to return to our "'Ace Tomato' designer" screen. We can then just replace "Ace Tomato" with the next employer on our list, BiffCo, to reduce unnecessary retyping of "designer." (Alternatively, if you have a slow Internet connection, just copy the word "designer" and paste it into the current screen any time it's needed to save time and frustration.) Either way, we'll end up with an Indeed.com screen that looks like this:

BiffCo designer	SEARCH

And we'll repeat the process until we've completely filled in our LAMP list Posting column for all targets.

Viewed another way, what we are doing in this process is first searching for jobs in the first row of the table below, followed by the middle row. If we find no results in the middle row, we know there's no match.

POSTING SCORE PROCESS FOR A GRAPHIC DESIGNER	
Employer & Keyword	3
Employer	2
No Match	1

This step moves fast if we stay focused; we can complete a forty-employer LAMP list in about fifteen minutes. We'll discuss how to sort our completed LAMP list shortly.

Are there alternatives to a 3-point rating scale for Postings? If so, when should I use them?

Yes, there are. Use the criteria in the table to determine whether the standard 3-point Posting rating scale or an alternative will work best for your LAMP list:

MAX SCORE IN POSTING COLUMN	WHO SHOULD USE IT	WHY?
2	Small-company job seekers; entrepreneurs	Roles are less defined in smaller organizations; any opening is a plus
3	Everyone else	Highlights relevant postings at maximum speed
4	Undergraduate intern seekers; common professional degree holders (MBAs, RNs)	"Intern" and degree name (if common in postings) are excellent search terms—use 4-point scale if one or the other is relevant, and 5 if both are
5	Internship seekers among those pursuing professional degrees (first-year MBAs)	"Intern" and degree name (if common in postings) are excellent search terms—use 4-point scale if one or the other is relevant, and 5 if both are

WHEN TO USE ONLY A 2-POINT SCALE IN YOUR POSTING COLUMN

Those targeting start-ups or small employers (two to ten employees) should rate their employers using only 1s and 2s in their Posting column. To do this, search *only* on the employer's name (no keywords), and give the employer a Posting score of 2 if *any* postings are available and 1 if not.

At very small employers, an employee will likely need to wear many hats, doing whatever needs to be done most at a given moment.

Therefore, titles are both less formal and less standardized than at larger employers, so if this is your search, save yourself some click-throughs and focus on speed—especially because those firms are less likely to post jobs in the first place!

Finally, if you are uncertain about what your job-specific keyword should be given the nature of your search, use a 2-point system. Some job seekers simply have no reliable keyword for the particular position they're after. If this is true for you, use the simplest possible system to separate those employers that are hiring from those that aren't.

One job seeker I worked with had a graduate degree in environmental management, and she sought jobs in either consulting or project management at the energy and utility companies she was targeting. There was simply no keyword that would help her quickly identify a specific relevant posting, so she just noted whether the targets had postings at all (making that employer's Posting score a 2) or not (a 1 in that case).

Motivation will always be our most important criterion for choosing a target employer, so although a current posting is nice to have, it's not a must-have. Therefore it is OK to trade quality for speed at this stage if we don't have keywords that allow us to classify those postings efficiently right now. Once we complete our list and identify our top employers by Motivation, we will go back and review postings in more detail.

WHEN TO USE A 4-POINT SCALE IN YOUR POSTING COLUMN

Use a 4-point scale for Postings if you are an undergraduate seeking an internship or a graduate of a popular professional or specialty degree program (where the degree name is likely to be a keyword in the job posting itself).

For undergraduates seeking internships, recall that the word "intern" is a very restrictive search term in Indeed.com (see page 32). Thus it is great for identifying ideal 4-point postings, but it should be the first word to omit if you get zero results. In other words, if you get zero results, you will proceed by just returning to the 3-point system we described earlier. Higher Posting scores will still represent more time-sensitive opportunities.

If, in our Ace Tomato example from earlier, we were seeking an internship in graphic design rather than a full-time job, our search would appear as shown in the table below.

POSTING SCORE PROCESS FOR A GRAPHIC DESIGNER SEEKING INTERNSHIP	
Employer & Keyword & Intern	4
Employer & Keyword	3
Employer	2
No Match	1

The theory is that an employer who is trying to hire a full-time graphic designer right now would be more interested in a graphic design intern than an employer who is not. Thus, although in our example we would consider an internship posting ideal (a 4), a relevant full-time posting is the next best thing (a 3). Meanwhile, any hiring at all (a 2) is better than nothing (a 1).

For professional or specialty degree holders, use a slightly different approach. For this example, let's discuss the case of Amy, a registered nurse (RN) seeking a home care position because she prefers it to working in a hospital. She should switch the order of her search terms so that her degree is the second most important keyword.

For example, if the first employer in her LAMP list is MediVisitPlus, a company providing a variety of healthcare services, her "what" field in Indeed.com might look like this:

MediVisitPlus RN "home care"	SEARCH

If she found relevant postings using that search, she would give MediVisitPlus a Posting score of 4. If not, she'd want to see whether they had openings for any of their other groups to assess their hiring activity in general. Thus, she'd try:

MediVisitPlus RN	SEARCH

And with that, Amy would return to the 3-point process. In essence, all we're doing in a 4-point Posting rating system is adding an extra keyword. However, in this case, the degree is more common than the job preference keywords ("home care"), so Amy should leave it in the search box longer; the resulting Posting score process would look like this:

POSTING SCORE PROCESS FOR AN RN SEEKING HOME CARE NURSING POSITION	
Employer & Degree & Keyword	4
Employer & Degree	3
Employer	2
No Match	1

Once again, the higher the Posting score, the more time-sensitive the opportunity. In Amy's case, seeing an RN posting for a home care position is her ideal (a 4), but any RN hiring even outside the home care group (a 3) is better than unrelated positions like accounting or human resources (a 2) or no hiring at all (a 1).

WHEN TO USE A 5-POINT SCALE IN YOUR POSTING COLUMN

The 5-point Posting rating system simply combines the two cases examined in the 4-point situation—professional students seeking internships. I'd recommend a 4-point scale for a graduating MBA student, but a first-year MBA student seeking a marketing internship (let's call him Jake) would use the 5-point process shown in the following table:

POSTING SCORE PROCESS FOR AN MBA STUDENT SEEKING MARKETING INTERNSHIP	
Employer & Degree & Keyword & Intern	5
Employer & Degree & Keyword	4
Employer & Degree	3
Employer	2
No Match	1

In other words, if ShoeCo, an athletic apparel company, is at the top of his LAMP list, Jake would start with the following list of search terms in Indeed.com:

ShoeCo MBA marketing intern	SEARCH

If he didn't find any postings using all of those search terms, Jake would omit the word "intern" and repeat the search to see whether ShoeCo should receive a Posting score of 4. Although those job postings wouldn't be ideal hits, they would let Jake know that ShoeCo does hire for relevant positions full-time, giving him two key pieces of information:

- ShoeCo is more likely than firms that are not posting MBA marketing positions to have an MBA marketing internship at some point.

- Even if Jake doesn't get an internship after networking with ShoeCo this year, it may help him get a job after graduation next year (and thus the time spent would not be "wasted").

If once again there were no hits, Jake would want to know whether ShoeCo does *any* MBA hiring by searching the following terms:

ShoeCo MBA	SEARCH

If relevant hits were found for these search terms unlike the others (such as "Corporate Finance Associate"), Jake would give ShoeCo a Posting score of 3 and learn two *other* pieces of information:

- ShoeCo is financially healthy enough to afford hiring MBAs in the current economy.

- ShoeCo values the MBA degree more than firms who do not specify this degree in a job posting.

If there are no postings for that search, Jake would see whether ShoeCo has any online job postings available whatsoever to earn a Posting score of 2 (indicating that at least they are not under a total hiring freeze). If not, ShoeCo would get a 1.

Using Google Reader, I can subscribe to RSS feeds that automatically update me when new job postings become available for certain search terms. Should I subscribe to these?

If you understand half of those references, then you are ahead of the game! If you don't, that's OK. Using RSS feeds is a very efficient way to conduct a reactive search—one in which you wait for postings to go live and then reach out to the employers in question (or apply directly). However, I don't advocate this approach, precisely *because* it is reactive.

Postings are nice information to have, but Motivation is ultimately the most important driver of this process, as you'll see shortly. Getting Posting information once, up front, as a "snapshot-in-time" is ideal, because this process is designed to help you execute a *proactive* plan for your top-choice employers *right now*.

Constantly rechecking for new postings takes you away from proactive execution of a strategy and back toward a reactive, shotgun approach to the job search. Therefore, I do not recommend using RSS feeds at this time.

Once I complete my list, how do I sort it?

If all goes well, our list should finally end up looking something like this (for illustration purposes, let's assume we used a 5-point Posting rating system):

#	LIST	ALUMNI	MOTIVATION	POSTING
1	Ace Tomato Co.	Y	4	3
2	BiffCo	Y	5	5
3	Darlington Electronics	N	4	4
4	Hanso Corporation	Y	3	2
5	Initech	N	1	5
...	...	...	...	...
...	...	...	...	...
...	...	...	...	...
39	Staypuft Marshmallow Inc.	N	5	5
40	Zamunda Airlines	Y	1	1

With that, our Posting column is completed! All that remains to do is to sort the list and ensure that it is ordered properly. We'll cover this in a brief Step 1 wrap-up section at the end of this chapter—but for now, some congratulations are in order. You've compiled all of the raw data necessary to complete your very first LAMP list!

L	A	M	P
✓	✓	✓	✓

TROUBLESHOOTING

My profession (for example, venture capital) tends not to post jobs online. Can I skip this step?

If you found during the L step of this process that Indeed.com did not help you find any relevant postings, you may skip this step and fill in all of your selections as 1s. This essentially cancels it as a prioritization factor, so you'll be relying only on Motivation and Alumni, but the process is still fundamentally the same, even if your entire Posting column is all 1s.

My profession has specific job posting websites targeted to people in my desired profession (for example, philanthropy.com for nonprofit jobs)—are those websites better for this step than Indeed.com?

In my experience, Indeed.com tends to find all of the same postings (and more) than more targeted websites, so I'd say stick with Indeed.com. However, these specific job search engines may offer more guidance for the families of jobs available in that industry.

If you have doubts, investigate it this way: find a few interesting postings on your alternative website and cross-check them with Indeed.com. If Indeed.com finds everything you found, stay with Indeed.com. However, if it missed any critical postings or if the alternative site's search guidance proves helpful, feel free to use that instead for this step.

Remember that the goal for this step is to estimate the *urgency* of getting in touch with a particular target based on their current hiring activity, so whichever website best helps you accomplish this is the one you should go with.

Indeed.com didn't find any postings for one of my targets, but that target has job postings on its website! What gives?

Sadly, this will happen occasionally. Neither Indeed.com nor any other job search engine is perfect. Job search engines essentially use Google in tandem with their own methodologies to look for postings featuring your search terms. However, Google itself requires that a website meet some minimum threshold of popularity before it will be "found." Thus if one or more of your target employers are not heavily trafficked online, Indeed.com may not add a lot of value. This is absolutely fine for right now. We are just assessing whether the employer has any *easy-to-find* postings. If it doesn't, but we later determine that that employer is a top target, we'll find those relevant postings (for example, on the employer's own modest-but-functional website) soon enough.

If you search for jobs on LinkedIn and it doesn't find any, it automatically checks SimplyHired as a backup search—isn't this better than Indeed.com?

I actually had one student test this very hypothesis. His assessment was that Indeed.com found more postings than the combination of LinkedIn and SimplyHired, in part because Indeed.com searches LinkedIn as part of its search. Furthermore, Indeed.com completes its search more quickly, because it searches all locations at once, rather then sequentially as LinkedIn/SimplyHired does; SimplyHired is searched only after LinkedIn fails to find anything. This results in a ten- to twenty-second search to reveal no hits instead of a one- to two-second search on Indeed.com, which vastly increases the likelihood of cognitive drift and distraction.

Indeed.com doesn't seem to find any results for any of my targets, so my P column is full of 1s—should I try other websites?

Some professions, like law, tend not to post jobs in large numbers—thus most of your results for the P column may be 1s. That said, even if only 5 to 10 percent of your targets have hiring activity right now, that information is crucial for helping you create your order of attack. Other firms *may* be

continued

TROUBLESHOOTING

hiring right now, but it's better to start with the firms you're *certain* are hiring right now.

Even if none of your targets has relevant postings, at worst you are out fifteen minutes of time if you stay disciplined. You'll also have some peace of mind that no one on your employer list is being disproportionately targeted by other job searchers right now.

However, if your first 25 percent of targets do not show up in Indeed.com, I'd advise you to simplify your rating system (for example, from a 3-point scale to a 2-point one). This will speed up this step while simultaneously verifying that your search terms are not overly restrictive. Remember that one employer's "computer programmer" may be another employer's "software consultant"!

If Indeed.com is not returning what you consider a satisfactory number of results, I wouldn't try searching again on a different job search engine. Doing so usually exceeds the "point of diminishing returns"—a term for when results achieved from additional effort simply aren't worth the time and energy required.

Step 1 Wrap-Up

Our LAMP list is now completely filled in, but we must take a moment to finalize it before moving forward.

First, we're going to sort your list again. To do this in your spreadsheet, follow these steps:

1. Highlight your entire LAMP list.

2. Select Sort (which is often located in a drop-down menu called Data or Tools). A window will open and ask which criteria you would like to sort your list by. In this window, set your priorities in this order:

   a) Top priority: sorting the Motivation column's values from Largest to Smallest—meaning that your 5s, or dream employers, should always be at the top of your LAMP list.

   b) Second priority: sorting the Posting column's values from Largest to Smallest. (In some software packages, you'll need to "add a level" of sort prioritization to do this.) This will identify which employers within a certain Motivation category are most time-sensitive.

   c) Third priority: sorting the Alumni column's values in descending order from Z to A (reverse alphabetically). This means that if all other information is equal, employers with Ys in their Alumni column will be listed before those with Ns.

The final version of your Sort dialog box should look like this before clicking OK (image taken from Microsoft Excel):

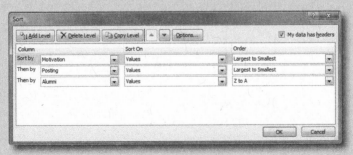

continued

Following those steps will give you a sorted LAMP list that looks like this:

#	LIST	ALUMNI	MOTIVATION	POSTING
1	BiffCo	Y	5	5
2	Staypuft Marshmallow Inc.	N	5	5
3	Darlington Electronics	N	4	4
4	Ace Tomato Co.	Y	4	3
5	Hanso Corporation	Y	3	2
...	...	...	...	...
...	...	...	...	...
...	...	...	...	...
39	Initech	N	1	5
40	Zamunda Airlines	Y	1	1

This sorting helps us with our second housekeeping task: order verification.

At the start of this LAMP process, I mentioned that the goal was to give you an ordered list of targets so that your most important and promising employers were addressed first—thus, if you had time to approach only five, you'd be approaching the top five on your list; if you had time to approach only ten, you'd approach employers ranked 1 to 10 on your list; and so on.

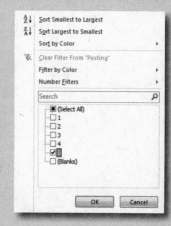

To verify your list's order, there are two steps.

First, apply a data filter to your LAMP list by highlighting your entire list and choosing your spreadsheet's Filter option (also often located in a menu labeled Data). This allows you to choose certain values for a column, and all rows of data not matching that value will be hidden from view temporarily. Filter first on the maximum value you awarded for your Postings (for example, any 5s, using a 5-point rating scale) and click OK, as in the image on the previous page.

After clicking OK, you should see only employers to whom you awarded the highest possible Posting score.

Next, review the list of visible targets and ask yourself (honestly, now)—does knowing that these employers have a job posting that is both current and relevant change your motivation to approach them? *If so, increase your Motivation score by a half a point, a full point, or even more to reflect your newfound motivation.* This will move that employer higher on your list.

Many job seekers *do* find employers more enticing when they know an open position exists there right now. If you share this perspective, modify your Motivation score, *provided it means you have an increased willingness to apply effort toward them.* Ultimately, this list is designed to ensure that your targets are ordered correctly, and sometimes that involves manual adjustments.

Next, we will do something similar with our Motivation column:

1. Remove the filter on the Posting column so all of your targets are displayed once again.

2. Filter your LAMP list so only employers to whom you assigned a Motivation score of 1 appear (meaning they are unknown to you).

3. If any of the filtered employers now offer a positive indication of employment—in other words, a highly rated Posting or a Y in the Alumni column—spend ONE MINUTE MAXIMUM PER EMPLOYER Googling them to find out what they do and where they are located.

4. If in that minute you become more interested in that employer, increase your Motivation score accordingly. (You can increase that employer's Motivation to 2 points or, if they become a new favorite, all the way to 5.)

continued

The rationale behind this step is that any employers that you gave a Motivation score of 1 to may have low brand awareness and thus may not get approached by job seekers very often. Therefore, they are likely to welcome any proactive attention they do get from job seekers. This gesture alone can gain you instant consideration for open positions, present or future.

Note that in our completed table on page 71, both Initech and Zamunda Airlines would qualify for additional investigation—the former for its top-rated posting, and the latter for its Y in the Alumni column.

Finally, we'll sort our list again, just as we did before: by Motivation, Posting, and Alumni, in that order. This will ensure that your Top 10 targets according to your LAMP list truly feature your Top 10 favorite potential employers. With this step completed, our LAMP list is officially done!

From here on out, your LAMP list will be the game plan you follow for the rest of the process. Whenever it is time to initiate outreach to new targets, you'll refer to your LAMP list to see who's next on the list—no anxiety, no decision making required.

A very common job search mistake is to use spreadsheets for both keeping a target employer list *and* tracking outreach. This makes job seekers *hate* their spreadsheets, and I don't want you to hate your LAMP list. It represents the myriad possibilities your life has yet to offer; it should be a document that represents hope and motivation rather than overwhelming work and oppressive deadlines. Frankly, you've done the hardest work already—you've opened your mind to what you want next out of life and to an organized process for getting yourself there. Your stress over this process is done—from here on out, it's just implementation, and we're going to let our email program's calendar suffer through the majority of that for us!

L	A	M	P
✓	✓	✓	✓

CONTACT:
Boosters, Obligates, and Curmudgeons

CHAPTER 5

NATURALIZE

What do you mean by "Naturalize"?

In this chapter, I'll teach you how to "create" contacts at top-priority employers where you were unable to find them initially.

Naturalization typically refers to the process by which someone becomes a citizen of a country by means other than birth, but in general the term means to adapt something to a new environment. In the 2-Hour Job Search, to *naturalize* means to turn an N into a Y in your Alumni column. We will do this by using means other than our most recent alumni database to identify potentially sympathetic contacts.

Looking back at our completed LAMP list example on page 71, we see that only three of our top five have Ys in the alumni column: Ace Tomato, BiffCo, and Hanso Corporation. For those employers, nothing further is required in this chapter, because we already have one or more "starter contacts" to begin the outreach process with (we'll discuss exactly how to do this in chapter 6).

In total, Step 2: Contact will take 50 minutes, broken down as follows:

	TIME REQUIRED
Chapter 5: Naturalize	20 minutes
Chapter 6: Email	20 minutes
Chapter 7: Track	10 minutes
Total for Step 2	50 minutes

The critical goal for Step 2: Contact is to identify and secure conversations with potential advocates at our top target employers as efficiently and effectively as possible. The specific goal of this chapter is to find an alternative starter contact at our other two top hypothetical targets—Staypuft Marshmallow and Darlington Electronics.

(Note: If you have Ys for all of your Top 5 in your LAMP list, that's great news! Skip ahead to chapter 6, as this content doesn't apply to your search quite yet. If later in this process you encounter a top-priority target that has an N in the Alumni column, come back and read this then when it is more relevant.)

Isn't this inefficient? Why didn't we find these contacts during the Alumni step?

Had we tried to Naturalize contacts during Step 1, we would have wasted a lot of time searching for contacts *we'd never actually use* at employers we frankly don't care that much about.

The crucial difference between then (when we filled in the Alumni column) and now is that *now* we know which employers are worth the additional effort. Naturalizing contacts can be time-consuming— converting a stranger into an advocate requires some effort. Thus we want to do this only when we don't have an easier option available (and even then only for employers we've determined are top targets). Our LAMP list gives us this precise information.

Employers are not children, so you don't have to love them all equally! We're effectively co-opting the airline industry's discovery from the 1980s that not all of their customers were equally profitable. Treating certain ones better than others was actually quite profitable, and establishing "frequent-flier" programs allowed the airlines to more quickly recognize which customers deserved greater investment. These investments ranged from material perks like complimentary business-class upgrades to service perks like early boarding and priority status when flying standby on full flights.

In effect, the airlines themselves applied the 80-20 Rule to find that 80 percent of their profits came from 20 percent of their customers—specifically, those that traveled most frequently and those that bought the more expensive business-class and first-class tickets. Businesses can actually *lose* money on some customers, so airlines are willing to alienate the occasional college student who buys a rock-bottom weekend fare if this preferential treatment keeps the travel-every-week consultant happy.

Our LAMP list has basically helped us determine who our "most valued customers" are. We won't ignore all the other target employers in our list, just as airlines won't refuse to sell airline tickets to college students, but we're certainly going to give more attention to our top targets. The first form of this greater level of attention is the willingness to use more time-consuming measures to find contacts when necessary.

So when necessary, how *do* I find alternative starter contacts?

The short answer is "systematically," just like everything else in this process. Contacts can be found for *any* employer, given enough time—the challenge is to find one efficiently.

What I had you do in the Alumni column of your LAMP list was to use the most efficient source of contacts—your most recent alumni database—as a starting point. However, when that approach fails, it is critical to try the second most efficient source of contacts next, followed by the third, and so on. The good news is that this ranking of contact source efficiency already exists. The bad news (for me, at least) was that I had to create it myself from many hours of trial and error with many different job seekers.

Before I share with you my algorithm for efficiently and systematically converting Ns into Ys in the Alumni column, let me just add that this is officially my *absolute favorite* step to help job seekers with.

As a kid I loved the Encyclopedia Brown and Two-Minute Mysteries book series. Both were collections of short mysteries that crafty readers could solve themselves using the clues provided, if they were attentive and clever enough. Helping job seekers naturalize contacts reminds me of puzzling over those mysteries, trying to find the mistake the criminal made that allowed his or her capture. Finding contacts is nothing more than a bit of amateur detective work, and you'll be amazed (and likely a bit disturbed, too) at how much you can learn about people these days, armed with only the Internet, a logical approach, and a bit of creativity.

Now that we know which top targets don't have ready-made contacts from our most recent alumni database, we'll use the following hierarchy to seek alternative starter contacts until we find a hit (and if you process all of your Top 5 employers with Ns in the Alumni column simultaneously, this step should take you only fifteen minutes):

1. Most recent alumni database (*already done*)

2. Undergraduate alumni database (if different)

3. LinkedIn

4. Facebook

5. Fan Mail

6. LinkedIn backsolving

7. Cold calls

As we go lower on the list, the average rate of return of the method gets smaller, and we want to use the method with the highest average rate of return available to us at any given time.

What is "average rate of return"?

An average rate of return is the amount of benefit you expect to gain per unit of investment (be it time, money, or even attention). For example, imagine that you and I play a game in which we bet $1 on a coin flip—let's say that you take heads, and I take tails. Each time we played one of us would win a dollar and the other would lose a dollar, and if we played the game many times (let's say a million), we'd win about as often as we lost, meaning we'd break about even. Thus our average rate of return for this game is $0 per play.

Alternatively, let's pretend that I offered to play a different game with you. In this game, you would pay me $1 every time a 1, 2, 3, 4, or 5 was rolled on a six-sided die (which is in no way rigged or tampered with), but every time a 6 came up I would pay you $10,000. Would you want to play?

Yes, absolutely you would. Unfortunately I can't afford to play that game with you, because it would put me out of house and home very quickly! Although you would "lose" this game a majority of the time, the benefit from winning is so high that you can afford to lose hundreds of times in a row before winning just once and turning a significant profit.

If we played this dice game six hundred times, on average you would win one hundred times (for a profit of a cool one million dollars!) and lose five hundred times (for a loss of $500) for an average profit of $999,500. If we played this game just six times, on average you would win once (for $10,000) and lose five times (for a loss of $5), yielding a profit of $9,995.

Specifically, the average rate of return refers to the average outcome per game, no matter how many times you play (be it six hundred, six million, or just once). Each time we play this game, on average you'd win (and I'd lose) about $1,665.83, making this your (very handsome) average rate of return.

What does "average rate of return" have to do with finding alternative starter contacts?

Each of those methods I just listed requires different amounts of time and effort to execute, and that time and effort is part of the average rate of return calculation. For example, Fan Mail, which you'll learn about shortly, has a very high rate of success in terms of getting a response, but it requires significantly more time than the methods ranked above it. As a result, Fan Mail's average rate of return per minute of job search time required is actually lower than the methods above it, making it a less desirable option than using LinkedIn or Facebook, for example.

Now let's discuss each of the methods in descending order of their average rate of return:

MOST RECENT ALUMNI DATABASE

This is what we used to fill in our Alumni column in the first place. No further discussion is required.

UNDERGRADUATE ALUMNI DATABASE

Typically, job seekers get closer to their preferred career with each new degree earned, making more recent alumni databases more relevant than older ones. However, alumni databases are generally very easy to navigate and allow you to contact fellow alumni directly, making them excellent for our purposes.

This will be a great option for those of you who attended large state schools for your undergraduate studies, as the alumni databases are likely to be quite large. However, for those of you who attended small undergraduate schools (as I did) or international universities, this option will have a lower expected value. But because checking these databases takes only a few seconds—really, just the time it takes to log in—their speed makes them a great second option.

Spend no longer than three minutes on this effort; if you don't have immediate access to your undergraduate alumni database, simply move on. You can request it later in the process while waiting for your first batch of contacts to respond to your outreach emails (the subject of the next chapter).

LINKEDIN

I don't endorse a lot of career-related websites, but I consider LinkedIn a must. Even better, it's free. It is essentially a professional version of Facebook (which we'll discuss later in this chapter), using social network technology to help you find connections that match your needs or interests through your professional network of colleagues.

LinkedIn is essentially "six degrees of separation" for your job search. Supply LinkedIn with the name of an employer, and it returns to you the closest connections you have to someone who works there. LinkedIn uses several different classifications to describe the nature of your connection, so before I describe each in detail, I'll list them for you in decreasing order of helpfulness:

- First-degree connections
- Second-degree connections
- Group connections
- Third-degree connections
- No connection

First-degree connections are ideal—someone from your immediate network (people who either have accepted your invitation to link or have invited you to link) works there. They either switched jobs without your knowing it, or you just plain forgot where they worked. Regardless, refinding them at a target employer is an ideal scenario. If necessary, rekindle the friendship (the best practice is to acknowledge the gap in communications and cite any specific reasons for it, like grad school or new parenthood) and ask whether they'd be interested in catching up by phone. This will be a better venue for assessing their willingness to help than asking right out of the gate in an email for help with employment.

Second-degree connections are the next best thing. One of your first-degree connections knows someone employed at your target employer. Reach out to your first-degree connection and ask them to make an introduction for you to your potential contact. LinkedIn does allow you to reach out to that contact directly via their website, but I discourage this—the first thing that contact will do is ask your mutual colleague what they think of you before responding, so you want to make sure your colleague is warmed up and comfortable endorsing you before moving forward.

In addition, it's just classy to keep your immediate network in the loop and much more personal than a website-facilitated email, which to me smacks of the social awkwardness of a collect call (for those of you who've known only cellphones, back in the era of home telephones calls were only charged to the caller unless they were made "collect," meaning the caller would ask the call recipient to pay for it).

Group connections are the minimum connection level I'd pursue on LinkedIn. For such connections, LinkedIn will usually offer you only the person's first name and last initial plus employer and job title. A simple Google search on their first name, employer, and job title will often furnish you with the last name, and some clever Google detective work will usually help you backsolve into their likely email address.

An amazing website called Emails4Corporations (http://sites .google.com/site/emails4corporations) will help you puzzle together email addresses at many (especially larger) employers by providing you with that employer's email convention, such as firstname_ lastname@company.com. In addition, this website provides a great resource for sourcing new employers, as it offers prepared lists of employers matching commonly sought criteria—"Consumer Packaged Goods companies in the Bay Area," for example. If this doesn't work, searching an employer's "Contact us" section may also give you the email naming convention that you can try first in order to avoid LinkedIn's comparatively impersonal infrastructure. If you're wrong, the email bounces back immediately and you know where you stand, so time lost to guessing incorrectly is minimal.

Group connections are similar to alumni connections in that you have no mutual contacts, but your shared interest alone may pique their interest enough to make them open to an informational interview request. (In some cases, you may find literal alumni through a group connection on LinkedIn that doesn't show up in your alumni database, simply because professionals tend to be more vigilant about updating their LinkedIn information than their alumni database records!) A quick Google search of their names may give you an article you can use as an icebreaker, as well. That said, Group connections are the minimum "connection strength" I'd consider a match for connection purposes.

Third-degree connections are employees of your target employer who know someone who knows someone who is in your immediate network. Frankly, it's a stretch to call these people connections at all. Because reaching out to these individuals requires the use of LinkedIn's infrastructure for emailing, and you have to pay for this service (although the first few may be free), I don't find it worth the time or effort.

Similarly, finding no connections at all means that for reaching this employer, LinkedIn is a dead end. Move on down the list to Facebook.

To summarize, what you're seeking on LinkedIn are first-degree connections, second-degree connections, or Group connections when your alumni databases have not provided you with a relevant contact at a top target. The added benefit of having someone vouch for you in the second-degree connection case is outweighed by the additional amount of time and effort it takes to enlist a colleague's help; that is why it appears below alumni databases in my algorithm, due to its lower expected value per minute of effort required.

So how do I find these contacts in LinkedIn?

To use LinkedIn most efficiently, go straight to its Advanced People search option—as of this writing, located in the upper-right corner of the home page. This leads you to a page that looks like this:

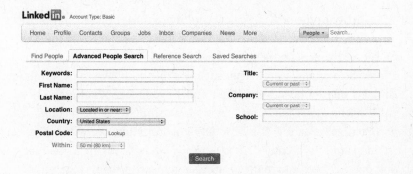

Insert the target employer's name into the Company field and in the "Current or past" dropdown box choose "Current"—this eliminates people who previously worked for that employer from your search results. Although those people might indeed be helpful, they are far less likely to be helpful than current employees are, either because they have a dated network there or because they have mixed feelings about re-engaging with a previous employer. Using the 80-20 Rule, former employees simply don't offer as good a return on your effort as current ones, so let's focus our attention there.

Click "Search." If you find very few hits, choose your first option using the following criteria (in order):

1. Closeness of connection—first-degree connections over second-degree, for example.

2. Relevance of targeted contact to desired career path.

3. Currentness of the connection—that is, how close your mutual contact is in the case where you have multiple second-degree connections.

4. Experience of target contact—several years more than you is ideal; that means the person is experienced enough to have a network of influence, but not so high up as to potentially have no time for you. (That said, recognize that upper management can hand you off in a way that junior employees can't!)

Start with the best contact according to these criteria, and move on down your list. If you find many hits (twenty-five to fifty or more), add your school's name to the "School" field of the Advanced People Search and search again. It's possible you have some alumni contacts there who simply didn't update your school's alumni database or who didn't join your school's LinkedIn Group (both common occurrences). Barring any first-degree connections you find, these "hidden alumni" second-degree or group connections are a great second option, thanks to many alumni's tendency to want to help their own kind.

One final note—once you find a contact on LinkedIn that you think looks promising, write down the person's name and position in a blank email and save just that information as a draft (this goes for contacts found using any subsequent methods as well, except you would also include any relevant website references). These contacts are harder to retrieve than ones from alumni databases, but adding their information to your LAMP list doesn't add value—your Drafts email folder is a far more efficient place to store contact information, and it adds a sense of urgency to actually getting that email sent, rather than saving that information for a yet-to-be-determined time in the future. The future is now!

FACEBOOK

True, Facebook is more a social networking website than a professional one, but its long odds of success are counteracted by the minimal effort required and potential gigantic payoff. Essentially, this step involves posting a Facebook status update asking your friends whether anyone knows anyone at your target company (Darlington Electronics, for example).

This takes mere seconds, but it could give you exactly what you're looking for. However, you should use this strategy judiciously; use it too frequently (daily or several times a week) and you could alienate your friends. Thus you want to first make sure there are no obvious contacts you're overlooking.

Using Facebook during the Naturalization process makes use of a concept identified by Stanford sociologist professor Mark Granovetter. He called it "the strength of weak ties" in a paper he authored back in 1973—decades before Facebook itself![1] The theory behind the strength of weak ties is that very close friends tend to share social networks, making them relatively redundant in the world of the job search. Furthermore, LinkedIn, being primarily a tool for professionals, links people in similar professions more frequently than not—again, causing social networks to overlap.

You may be connected to your weaker ties—your theater-major college roommate who now designs sets in Vermont, for example—on Facebook (a *social* network) but not on LinkedIn (a *professional* network). However, your ex-roommate's social network is likely to be *entirely* different from yours, given how much your lives have diverged over the last few years. Thus this "weak tie" is more likely than your closest friends to have a relevant contact you haven't already uncovered, and that person may be willing to give you a ringing endorsement due to the formative life experiences you shared. Similarly, that nice person you chatted with on an airplane, whom you expected never to see or hear from again but later found on Facebook, has an entirely different social network and may likewise be willing to connect you.

The strength of weak ties is a powerful concept in the job search—you simply never know. Thus a simple status update of "Can anyone put me in touch with someone from Darlington Electronics? In marketing, if possible?" could result in a plethora of offers, as it offers a wonderful chance to quickly reconnect and help a friend move forward in life. Altruism, a social norm rather than a market norm (and a concept that forms the backbone of the next chapter), is a powerful motivator.

The return on effort here has the potential to be massive—a relevant connection can be found in just seconds of effort. However, because this option is exhaustible, you should save it for situations when the more common approaches have failed—cases like Staypuft and Darlington Electronics, for which nothing has worked to date and the strength of those weak ties is needed most.

FAN MAIL

Fan Mail is essentially Google stalking, but with a nicer name. Thankfully, it's a skill most twenty- to thirty-somethings have practiced extensively by now, and for everyone else, it's never too late to start.

In Fan Mail, a job seeker will Google a set of terms designed to find off-the-beaten-path articles (especially interviews) with current employees of their targeted organizations at which they currently don't have contacts—in our example, Staypuft and Darlington Electronics. After finding those articles, the job seekers will reach out to the person interviewed, thank the person for specific insights the job seeker gleaned from that article, and ask for fifteen to thirty minutes of that person's time to discuss the topic in more detail and/or ask a few follow-up questions.

Finding an interview with a target employer's CEO or founder is fairly easy, but it is unlikely to warrant a response. These people have been interviewed dozens of times, their "comments" issued in press releases were most likely actually written by their public relations department, and their schedules do not often allow for unscreened informational interviews. No, your ideal target is the upper-middle manager who is just starting to get his or her name out there and become interesting and/or senior enough for media outlets to quote.

In both my own personal experience and that of my students, these people tend to be very excited to discuss their media appearance with a total stranger—perhaps the only thing better than being quoted in the media is talking to someone *about* being quoted in the media!

Employees at your targeted firms can burn out on informational interview requests based on only an alumni connection. This is not to say such requests are bad—their efficiency at attracting *the right kind* of contact (a population of contacts I call "Boosters," which we'll discuss in the next chapter) is by far the highest, which is why we use it as our first option in our LAMP list.

However, it is much more fun for employees to talk about their media interview than about the fact that you went to the same school and would now like their help. In addition, the fact that you found their interview indicates some minimum level of genuine interest in the firm, industry, and/or their experience, automatically separating you from a job seeker working only from knowledge gained in an alumni database.

If only Fan Mail were as efficient to implement as an alumni database, it would be the first option we'd resort to for our LAMP lists—however, its far greater prep time makes it an option we use only sparingly when needed, despite the very high response rate such outreach achieves.

So how do I write Fan Mail?

We'll actually be writing the email in the next chapter, so a better question is "How do I find a good contact using the Fan Mail approach?"

In early versions of the 2-Hour Job Search, I advised my job seekers to simply Google the employer's name, a keyword or two related to their job of choice (for example, "marketing" and "solar"), and the word "interview." This worked in some cases, but too frequently (especially for larger firms) it brought up lists of interviews with CEOs, CFOs, and the like about their company's quarterly results or annual shareholders' meeting.

It also brought up Google hits to job search websites that offer "insider" interview information about the employer, such as sample questions they have asked in the past during their interviews (which may or may not be used in the future or relevant to you). None of these websites actually helps you get that interview, so I advise my job seekers to avoid them altogether, given their limited value-add and massive potential for distraction.

And then along came a preposition. Nope, that's not a typo—I don't mean a "proposition." I mean a literal preposition—the word "with." Our goal in Fan Mail is to find less-mainstream interviews with people not commonly interviewed, who will therefore be flattered that their comments were deemed worth someone's time to read. (Mae West famously said, "Flattery will get you everywhere," and truer words have rarely been spoken.) These interviews usually appear in blogs, webzines, and less-formal magazines, and thankfully these all tend to share a particular convention—they all typically introduce their articles with the prefix "Interview with," making it the perfect block of text for Google searching blog, webzine, and magazine interviews.

So, to maximize your chance at finding a Fan Mail contact quickly, Google the target employer's name, a relevant keyword, and "interview with" (remembering to put quotes around those two words so they are searched as a single search term). If we return to our Staypuft example, it would translate to a Google search that looks like this:

Staypuft marketing "interview with"	SEARCH

This Google search will help filter out the CEO stockholder reports, the corporate press releases, and the job search websites offering interview hints for interviews it can't get for you—giving you the most direct access to interesting blog and magazine interviews with up-and-comers at your target organizations.

To me, the best part about this approach (in addition to the fact that it's simply fun to execute—like piecing together a puzzle) is that you learn something while you do it. Even if the first few interviews you click on aren't helpful, you're still internalizing relevant information about what is going on at that target employer. This information adds up over time. However, when you find that perfect Fan Mail interview, it feels like winning the lottery. You know that the person you're about to reach out to has most likely *never* had anyone write to ask him for further insight about his comments on that topic, so get ready to make someone's day. (He may make your career in return!)

The ideal article is one in which the person gives a unique, personal insight about a specific topic about which she has expertise. In an example I use when I present this content live, I use this technique to find a rather obscure blog interview with a marketing manager at a consumer technology firm; in it, he discusses his firm's expansion into Latin America, a brand-new market for them.

I'm not an expert in Latin America, nor am I an expert in his firm's technology, but that's what informational interviews are for! They help job seekers gain secondhand expertise by proxy, while thoroughly engendering goodwill with the person whose expertise they sought out. That is what makes Fan Mail outreach so powerful.

Once you find that perfect Fan Mail article, scour it for an email address of the person interviewed. You're much more likely to find one included with an informal online interview than with one in a more traditional medium. However, for those in which no contact information is included, I suggest you return to Emails4Corporations (see page 87) to see whether that offers an email address convention to try first. If that is unsuccessful, check the "Contact Us" section of the employer's website to see whether that helps before attempting a cold call to the company's main phone number.

All that said, Fan Mail is sadly not perfect—its downside is its incredible unpredictability. I've found perfect Fan Mail interview articles (including the contact's email address in the article itself!) with brand managers for NBA China in less than thirty seconds, yet I have also spent ten minutes trying to do the same for other target employers and have come up completely empty. Given this variance, my advice is to try to find Fan Mail articles for no more than five minutes before using the balance of your fifteen minutes designated for the Naturalize step on the next option, LinkedIn backsolving.

Fan Mail searches can become surprisingly addictive—it really does hurt to give up on one, particularly after one or more close calls with finding the right article. That is why it's essential to have a time limit on this step of the process, too.

LINKEDIN BACKSOLVING

LinkedIn backsolving is a hybrid approach between the LinkedIn and Fan Mail strategies.

"Backsolving" means using answers found later in a process to answer previously unsolved questions. My aforementioned trivia team uses the backsolving method at our weekly gatherings at Bull McCabe's. The final trivia round involves four general knowledge questions, followed by the final question, "What do the previous four answers have in common?"

In one recent match we were stumped by the first of the four questions—specifically, "This movie's sequel was *Demetrius and the Gladiators*—what was the original movie?" We had no idea. However, we solved the remaining three questions, whose answers were "Turkish" (the language spoken at the Hagia Sofia), "Bird" (jazz musician Charlie Parker's nickname), and "Steam" (a social networking and security software program created by the Valve Corporation). After we figured out that each of those three could be paired with the word "bath" to create a new word, such as "Turkish (bath)," "bird (bath)," and "steam (bath)," our team determined that "bathrobe" would be another possible answer. With that prompt, Hank the Savant recalled that the movie predecessor to *Demetrius and the Gladiators* was *The Robe*.

For job search purposes, backsolving means finding a contact who is likely to be relevant using information you can find in LinkedIn, and then Fan Mailing (aka Google stalking) her to see whether she has done any interviews featuring insights you could use as icebreakers in an informational interview request. This differs from the LinkedIn approach in that it doesn't rely on having a relevant contact to do the connection for you, and it differs from Fan Mail in that you are not searching for relevant industry interviews and mining them for potential contacts—instead, you are searching for potential contacts and mining them for relevant industry interviews you can turn into a good outreach email.

This approach can be as successful as Fan Mail, but because it effectively requires researching only one person at a time, it is a slower approach than Fan Mail and thus should be a near-last resort. The upside of this approach is that you can choose people with very relevant job titles to backsolve for. Sometimes LinkedIn will provide you with only a possible contact's job title, a first name, and last initial (or no name information at all)—however, the job title alone can be enough on which to base the search. For example:

Staypuft "Senior Marketing Manager" "interview with"	SEARCH

Again, as you get lower on the list of ways to find suitable starter contacts, the predicted return on your efforts decreases. LinkedIn backsolving is the final research-oriented approach I instruct my job seekers to employ before attempting a simple cold call, because it is speculative and can suck up hours of time following false leads if job seekers don't cap the amount of time they are willing to put toward it. Thus, if no contact is found within five minutes of attempting this method (which is enough time to try four or five different contacts or job titles you find in LinkedIn), put down the computer and pick up the phone.

COLD CALLS

These two words strike fear into the hearts of many job seekers, but I hope that by this point in the book they cause you to simply shrug your shoulders in response. When the worst an employer can do is ignore you (and by this point you've likely had some experience with that), it loses its power to intimidate.

When Internet research fails, I tell job seekers to call the main telephone line at the target employer and ask to speak to the most relevant contact they found using their previous methods. This approach is surprisingly effective at smaller companies with human receptionists—they may ask for your name, but rarely will they ask you for the purpose of your call before forwarding you on.

If you are asked, simply say you have some questions about Staypuft. Again, this approach has low odds of success because you have not been able to establish a common connection in advance, but cold calling is actually *faster* than both LinkedIn backsolving and Fan Mail, because a call like that can be done in under a minute. However, those cold calls are informed in part by information you gather in the preceding steps for finding alternative starter contacts, which is why it makes sense to leave it for last.

Do I have to do all of these steps for every one of my top targets?

Not at all! Remember that you use the methods we've covered only on an as-needed basis. Most of my job seekers never have to move beyond Fan Mail to find a good starter contact, so don't worry about doing everything all at once. It's very rare that any of my job seekers have had to resort to cold calls, and those occasions were mostly with very small employers—and they happened to be surprisingly successful.

Please just do your best to enjoy the process. It's business (more like a raffle, really), nothing more, so don't take any rejections personally. I don't particularly enjoy flossing, but I know doing so prevents cavities and that I hate getting dental work. In my mind, flossing isn't for me to like, it's for me to do. The down-the-road payoff is what makes the temporary inconvenience (or occasional cold call rejection) worthwhile.

And with that, we are done with the Naturalize portion of Step 2! Thus, it is now time to move on to the next step—emailing our newly found contacts. Ladies and gentlemen, prepare for liftoff!

TROUBLESHOOTING

I've tried all of the methods we've discussed here, but I still have not identified a contact—what do I do?

Sometimes certain top employers are very difficult to initiate contact with. This is through no fault of your own. However, your Fan Mail and LinkedIn backsolving skills will improve with time. So skip this employer for the moment and return to it after you've initiated outreach to your other Top 5 employers.

Once you get some practice under your belt, both with naturalizing contacts and with informational interviewing itself, you can return to this problematic employer for another try—that is, if your informational interviews haven't already yielded you a contact at this employer. Remember, we are trading comprehensiveness for speed in this process, so if *anything* bogs us down, it is best to move on. Sometimes a good night's sleep can make an answer clear to us in the morning; other times, fate will have a funny way of providing what you seek without warning. The important thing is always to keep moving forward. Information has a way of finding *you* once you know you need it, so set a reminder in your calendar program for two weeks out to try again.

## CHAPTER 6

THE 5-POINT EMAIL

 MINUTES

How does a 5-Point Email differ from any other outreach-oriented email?

The 5-Point Emails are shorter, relatively generic, and more efficient than other outreach emails, targeting those contacts that are most likely to provide you with real help in the job search. A job seeker need only keep five points in mind to create such an email. In this chapter, I'll teach you to do exactly that.

I think by now I know how to email people for job search help—it's getting them to *write me back* that's the problem. How do I do that?

This is the million-dollar question—and by far the most common complaint I hear from my job seekers about the search process. "Alumni never write me back." And I agree with them—no matter how customized your outreach, how flawless your prose, or how relevant your abilities, certain alumni will never write you back.

And that's OK. As you'll find out later, they are actually doing you a favor. The key is to target the right kind of alumni in your outreach, and that is what 5-Point Emails were invented to do.

So level with me—is this chapter going to tell me anything I don't already know?

Absolutely. In fact, employing the 2-Hour Job Search effectively requires forgetting everything you've ever learned about contacting someone for an informational interview, because technology has now rendered the long-standing conventional wisdom on this topic wrong and counterproductive.

Technology has fundamentally changed the way we interact with information. In the early days of email, back before "spam" referred to only a manufactured meat product rather than unwanted email, every email would actually be read. Today we can spend as much time cleaning out our inbox as we do reading messages. Instead of reading, as people used to, we now filter. If you want proof, pull up one of your favorite websites and see what's going on, just as you normally would.

Now that you've skimmed the page in your usual fashion, go back and look at the page again. I mean *really* look at it. The first time, did you even notice the banner ad at the top? The suggested purchases on the right? The various headers you rarely click on under the website's name? We ignore the vast majority of information we encounter—and the outreach emails we receive from job seekers are no exception.

Although technology has changed so much about the job search—twenty years ago, could we imagine the online job applications and job search engines that exist today?—the conventional wisdom has not changed. Therein lies the problem.

I went to college and to business school, and then became a career counselor myself, and throughout all of those years the conventional wisdom on requesting informational interviews was static, including tips like these:

- "Talk about your background, and relate it to that potential employer."

- "Tell the contact why their employer *in particular* is of great interest and a great mutual fit."

- "Customize your outreach for that specific employer— mention some specific research or news article about them you've recently discovered."

This conventional wisdom was so entrenched that even *I* endorsed it during my early years as a career coach, but conventional wisdom is very hard to buck for those on our side of the table as well! A couple of years in, though, I realized that although that advice may have worked when such requests were made via postal service or before spam cluttered our email inboxes, it doesn't now.

According to a 2008 Radicati Group study, 78 percent of all email sent that year was spam. For the typical user, four out of five emails should (rightfully) be ignored. Thankfully, email filters catch most of those these days, but we are still inundated by emails from people and organizations we *do* know. If your name isn't recognized by the recipient, your content needs to get to the point quickly. Spending precious words discussing your previous experience or including hyperlinks to other websites will likely result in your email getting deleted, unread, especially in an era when more and more emails are being read on smartphones and other mobile devices with screens designed for no more than a hundred words at a time.

Thus, in this chapter we're going to completely redesign the "traditional" outreach email and rebuild it from the ground up into something leaner, more efficient, and more effective. A key piece to making this possible is the recognition that all potential contacts are not created equal—some will be far more helpful than others. To maximize our efficiency, therefore, we need to target the right customer segment of contacts with the right kind of email.

What is a customer segment?

A customer segment is a subset of a population of customers (in this case, all potential contacts we may reach out to for help) that share characteristics in the way they interact with and consume a certain product. During my marketing days at General Mills, I learned that Cheerios had several distinct customer segments they specifically targeted: two of these segments were new parents and health-conscious adults.

New parents buy Cheerios as a way to show love and nurturing for their young children. (For many of these new parents, Cheerios were their own first solid food, so it becomes a tradition that gets handed down through generations.) Adding to their appeal for the new parent segment, Cheerios are highly portable—easy to put in a resealable plastic bag for on-the-go eating—and should any spills happen, they are simple to clean up. Plus, most young children really enjoy the taste and the fun "O" shape.

However, health-conscious adults couldn't care less about the easy cleanup and fun "O" shape. That customer segment buys Cheerios in order to reduce their cholesterol. On its box, Cheerios claims that its soluble fiber content is clinically proven to reduce a person's bad cholesterol as part of a heart-healthy diet.

These two target customer segments buy Cheerios for totally different reasons, but the result is the same: purchase. Thus commercials targeting the new parent segment may focus on the "nurturing" aspect of the product, whereas ads for cholesterol-concerned consumers may focus on its health benefits instead.

OK, so how does knowing about customer segments help me email potential job search contacts?

First, it alerts you to the fact that job search contacts can be segmented just as Cheerios shoppers can be. Different segments of alumni (in this chapter, I use this term to refer to both actual alumni and nonalumni contacts) respond to your outreach differently because each has different values and motivations—therefore, expecting all of them to respond to an outreach email in a similar fashion is unrealistic.

Through my experience over the years, I've identified three main customer segments of job search contacts. We'll discuss each of these segments in turn, starting with the one I mentioned at the beginning of this chapter.

If you recall, I agreed wholeheartedly that there is a segment of alumni who will never write you back, no matter how well crafted your email to them is. I call this segment Curmudgeons. Basically, Curmudgeons are the type of people who hate babies, kick puppies, ruin holidays, and so on.

OK, that's not all true. Curmudgeons can actually be wonderful people. However, they just happen to have *no* interest in helping you find a job, and this could be for any number of reasons. Maybe they don't enjoy their current job and are looking to leave it, maybe they didn't enjoy their experience at the school you have in common and want to disassociate from it, or maybe they just don't think talking to strangers about jobs is worth their time. Oddly enough, though, Curmudgeons are not the worst segment of contacts. At least they are up front about the fact they won't be helpful—unlike Obligates, our second (and worst) segment of contacts.

Whereas Curmudgeons are motivated by self-interest (in terms of time, emotional investment, or any other number of factors), Obligates are motivated by guilt. They perhaps benefited from the help of others when getting their last job, so now they feel obligated to do the same for someone else. However, they certainly don't *want* to, so they try to do just enough to relieve their guilt and get on with their day.

Obligates are the worst segment because the average rate of return when working with them is so perilously low. With Curmudgeons, you know within a couple of quick outreach efforts that they won't respond, so although you get no results, you've lost very little time and energy. Obligates, on the other hand, tend to consume *significant* amounts of your time and effort before revealing that they won't be very helpful. Perhaps they take a week to respond to your outreach email, or they need weeks to schedule an informational interview, or they cancel that informational interview at the last minute and then suddenly become very difficult to reschedule with.

The net result is that you as a job seeker spend a lot of time trying to connect with someone who doesn't genuinely want to connect with you. Unfortunately, Obligates frequently send mixed signals to job seekers. Remember, they are motivated by guilt, so they don't want the breakdown in the relationship to be *their* fault. However, they will take steps to either keep you at arm's length ("I don't have time for an informational interview, but send me your resume and I'll forward it on to some people.") or slow down the process enough that eventually you'll move on to someone else.

The 80-20 Rule applies once again in the networking phase of this process, because a vast majority of the help you receive in your job search will come from a minority of people. I call this third and final contact segment Boosters. Typically, Boosters love their current jobs and former schools, they genuinely enjoy helping people, and they appreciate the benefit of having a network of allies within their employers. Thus they enjoy engaging with people who take an interest in their careers.

The quintessential essence of a Booster is crystallized in a remark that one of my Duke MBA classmates made to me early in my job as a career coach: "If a student tells me they're from Fuqua, they automatically get fifteen minutes of my time."

That's it. No questions asked. He's already sold—he just needs to know what you're selling. *That's* a Booster—the person who has a lot of help to give, but nowhere to put it. Everything I teach you from this point forward is designed to appeal to Boosters. In fact, some of the techniques we'll employ are *specifically designed* to alienate Curmudgeons and Obligates.

Why would we want to alienate *anyone* in the job search?

I understand that this may seem bold or dangerous, but by definition Curmudgeons are never going to write back to us, no matter how personalized our outreach to them is, and we'd actually prefer that Obligates *not* write back to us, because the rate of return on our time invested in them is so low. The fewer Obligates we interact with, the more time we have for finding Boosters. Getting a job in an era in which hundreds of resumes get submitted overnight for a new job posting requires genuine human advocacy, and only Boosters provide that.

I know, you've been trained to write informational interview requests that attempted to appeal to everyone (using advice like I listed earlier), but I'm going to help you get more out of your outreach efforts by throwing all the old rules out the window and teaching you to write outreach emails specifically designed to appeal to Boosters. Boosters give us the highest rate of return—the most payoff with the least effort—so why not?

That said, maximizing our appeal to Boosters in an initial outreach email is a very different (and thankfully simpler!) process than writing an outreach email designed for anyone and everyone. To understand how to write such an email (the 5-Point Email that is the crux of this chapter), we must first learn how best to entice a stranger to help us move a couch.

Let me guess how—with lots and lots of money?

Yes. And no. It comes from an experiment conducted by my Fuqua colleague Dan Ariely, which he outlines in his book *Predictably Irrational*. In his study, an experimenter asked passersby to help him move a couch out of his moving truck under one of three conditions—for no compensation, for a small wage, and for a reasonable wage.

As you might guess, paying someone a reasonable wage for labor is an effective motivator. You might also assume that offering something is better than nothing; however, that's where you'd be wrong. Surprisingly, offering no compensation at all was just as effective as offering a reasonable wage, but offering only a small payment was less effective than either of the other scenarios!

Ariely contended that the introduction of monetary compensation into a request shifts the scenario from one based on a social norm (that is, a favor) to one based on a market norm (that is, work-for-hire). Philanthropy, he found, even on such a small scale, could be a very powerful motivator, but once money was introduced into the equation, *sufficient* money had to be offered to break even with the no-money scenario.

How does this relate to the job search?

Very simply, up to this point you've been taught to write informational interview requests using market norms—"Here's the value I'll bring to your company" and "Here's my background, which you should find compelling." In anything less than a stellar job market in which current employees get "finder's fees" for bringing in new employees, there is very little chance that any contact you reach out to will *ever* personally gain from helping you join his employer. In fact, he actually takes a risk by doing so, because if you turn out to be psychotic and make a bad impression on the senior person he handed you off to, his own reputation will suffer for having recommended you.

As Dan Ariely's experiment points out, once you introduce money into the equation, in order to be successful you have to pay enough for it to be worth someone's while, and I would argue that unless (and even then) you have experience directly related to the job you are attempting to network your way into, it will be nearly impossible for you to offer a "reasonable wage" that entices a contact to help you.

The real nugget in the study is the realization that social norms are so powerful. Better still, they attract the right kind of audience—people motivated by the self-esteem boost they get from helping others. Boosters, in other words.

Because it takes a good deal of money to match the efficacy of offering no money at all, I want you to write an outreach email that relies on social norms rather than market norms. This means cutting out everything about how the company will benefit from hiring you and how valuable your previous experience is. Keep in mind that advocacy matters more in today's job search than qualifications do.

Instead, I want your informational interview outreach email to rely on social norms rather than market norms—in other words, I want your outreach email to simply be an honest and concise request for a favor. To gain advocacy, this process needs to be about them, not you, and the 5-Point Email is the most efficient way to accomplish this.

So what exactly is a 5-Point Email?

It is an email written using five key points as guidelines, namely:

1. Fewer than 100 words
2. No mention of jobs anywhere (subject or body)
3. Connection goes first
4. Generalize your interest
5. Maintain control of follow-up

That first point may be a bit shocking. "Fewer than a hundred words?" Indeed, looking over your own previous informational interview request emails, you may see they are in the two-hundred-to five-hundred-word range. That's simply how many words it takes to employ the conventional wisdom of talking about your background, demonstrating some employer research, and guesstimating your value to an employer. However, that email might be incredibly tedious to read *even for you*—can you imagine receiving it from someone you don't even know? It would feel like she was trying to tell you why $1.05 should be sufficient motivation for you to help her move a couch!

Please remember that this is not your fault. You have been following well-entrenched conventional wisdom from well-trusted advisors. As I mentioned, I myself years ago gave this same off-kilter advice.

It took struggling over editing one too many four-hundred-word outreach emails as a career coach before I finally (and ashamedly) admitted, "I really don't want to read this." But if I didn't want to read it, and I was a career coach, who *would* want to read it?

Unlike me, the intended recipients of these emails did *not* earn their raises or promotions by helping out job seekers. During my corporate careers, before I became a career coach, I would simply glance at these messages to see whether the sender had a referral from anyone I knew and liked. If I didn't see that in the first few seconds, I would delete it and get back to work.

Even generous Boosters with time to burn would be better served by an email more suited to their "they automatically get fifteen minutes of my time" attitude. Lengthy outreach emails are a holdover from the envelope-and-stamp days when letters shorter than half a page might seem rude. However, the "kitchen sink" approach of including lots of information you want the recipient to know (without considering what your target audience *wants to hear*) and hoping he or she finds enough of it relevant to warrant a callback simply doesn't work in the age of smartphones and Twitter. Anything more than one hundred words from a stranger seems downright presumptuous. "Doesn't this job seeker know I'M A VERY BUSY PERSON?!"

Fine, then—show me one of these 5-Point Emails that does it all in fewer than one hundred words.

A totally fair request. Let's start with the original 5-Point Email. One of my original 2-Hour Job Searchers, Brooke, had completed her LAMP list, and she asked me how to maximize her chance at getting an informational interview. Again, I found myself armed with only conventional wisdom that I didn't even agree with myself, so we decided to create a new one from scratch. A template very similar to this one was the result, and it uses only ninety-one words in the body of the email:

SUBJECT: Duke MBA student seeking your advice

Dear Mr. Jones,

My name is Brooke Franklin, and I am a first-year Duke MBA student who found your information in the Duke alumni database. May I have 20 minutes to ask you about your experience with IBM? I am trying to learn more about marketing careers at technology companies in North Carolina, and your insights would be very helpful.

I recognize this may be a busy time for you, so if we are unable to connect by email I'll try to reach you next week to see whether that is more convenient.

Thank you for your time,

Brooke

Brooke and I knew that any outreach email had to be *short* in order to get read. An email this short can be viewed entirely in a single smartphone screen without scrolling, getting to the point quickly yet respectfully—exactly what a Booster would want to see.

In essence, the 5-Point Email is a document designed to maximize appeal to Boosters (our primary target) as efficiently as possible while inoculating against the most common reasons they might not respond. Each point of the 5-Point Email safeguards against a specific and common Booster concern.

The worst side effect of the old way's emphasis on "customizing" your outreach for different employers by talking about your past, et cetera, is that it eventually would get copied and pasted for other outreach emails. This is totally rational, as there simply isn't enough time to write three to four hundred unique words per contact. However, it was also completely transparent to job seekers' contacts that such "customized" emails were copy-and-paste jobs. Within just a handful of uses, what had originally been a genuinely personalized email became a long-form generic piece of spam.

Although the preceding email example may be rather generic in its own right, it is still better than the alternative. Without a doubt, short and generic is far better than *long* and generic. It gets to the point faster—"I need a favor—can you help me?"—which takes up less of a person's time and demonstrates appreciation for his busy schedule. As Thomas Jefferson wrote, "The most valuable of all talents is that of never using two words when one will do." I like to imagine that this initial outreach email is a proxy for what a project update email from this candidate (in a position working for my organization) might look like—is it straight and to the point, or does it meander before getting to the information that I really wanted to know hundreds of words ago?

Furthermore, by keeping your initial outreach under one hundred words, you're minimizing the chances that you'll (1) make grammatical and/or spelling mistakes or (2) accidentally alienate your Booster through your tone, word choice, or word count. More words may help you get a reluctant response from an Obligate or a magical connection with a Curmudgeon, but we are targeting Boosters—people who genuinely enjoy helping others. Therefore, there's no need to write more—in fact, writing more just means taking on unnecessary risk. Keep it short and move on.

Okay, so I understand the hundred-word limit now, but what about the second point? Why shouldn't I mention jobs in the email?

There are two main reasons not to do this: (1) it's unnecessary, and (2) it's intimidating.

It's unnecessary because they *already know* you're looking for a job.

How will they know that if I don't tell them so?

Because no sane person conducts informational interviews for fun! Everyone knows informational interview seekers are looking for jobs, which is totally fine. An informational interview request is a polite way to request a tryout with a Booster to see whether she might be willing to advocate for you within her organization.

So if they know I'm looking for a job, isn't it fake and awkward to ask them for an *informational interview* in the first place?

Of course it's fake and awkward—it's a job search! That doesn't mean it's not critical, however. They have information and connections you need, and most important, asking for the informational interview rather than a job is just plain good manners. To bring up jobs in your first email to a potential contact is like telling a dinner party host, "I brought you this bottle of wine in exchange for the dinner you'll be serving me later this evening." There's simply no need to be that blunt.

Just accept that the job search has some choreography to it, and your job is to execute your steps flawlessly. Being employed *anywhere* means dealing with awkward situations, and your ability to deal with this utterly predictable one is a potential Booster's best proxy for how well you'd deal with awkward situations on the job.

So I see why it's unnecessary, but why is mentioning jobs in the 5-Point Email *intimidating*?

Boosters want to help you, but their help is useful only if it's given voluntarily. One of the quickest ways to alienate a Booster is to ask for help before trying to get to know the person. After all, in informational interviews you are hoping that contacts are willing to put their reputation on the line (ever so slightly at times, substantially at others) to vouch for you to a peer or superior in their organization.

Before even Boosters are willing to do this, they must first develop a level of comfort and trust with you. Boosters are driven by the social norms of helping people in need. However, unlike in the Dan Ariely experiment case, Boosters do incur some risk by endorsing a candidate for a position. Thus, if you ask for their endorsement without getting to know them and giving them a chance to know you first, they may feel intimidated—as if by agreeing to conduct an informational interview with you, they are automatically signing on to help you find a job, regardless of how comfortable they are with you as a candidate. Therefore, they may choose to not respond at all.

Alternatively, you may get a Booster blow-off, which looks something like this: "Sorry, I don't know anything about any current openings—good luck!" Not even Boosters want to endure the awkwardness of telling job seekers outright that they need to get to know you (and you them) better before they decide whether or not to vouch for you and pass you on, so asking about jobs in that initial email is a quick way to lose a potentially excellent contact.

Some contacts may ask you to send your resume to them right away; they will forward it ahead on your behalf even without an informational interview. Unfortunately, this is typical Obligate behavior—they may indeed forward your resume on, and that is certainly better than nothing, but recognize that these Obligates certainly will not advocate for you—how could they, without knowing you at all? In other words, you get what you pay for, and "earning" a Booster requires a minimal investment of time getting to know him or her.

What if I've already identified a job posting at their employer? Should I mention this in my outreach email?

Yes. If you have conducted the legwork and already know the position that you think is the best fit for you online, mention it in your outreach email, such as in this example:

SUBJECT: Fuqua MBA student seeking your advice

Dear Mr. Jones,

My name is Javier Leon. I am a first-year Duke MBA student who found your information in the Fuqua alumni database. May I set up a phone call with you to discuss your experience with IBM? Your insights would be greatly appreciated, as I am now in the process of applying for an open marketing manager position there.

I recognize this may be a busy time for you, so if we are unable to connect by email I'll try to reach you next week to see whether that is more convenient.

Thank you for your time,

Javier

Recall that the 5-Point Email was designed to inoculate against reasons why a Booster may not want to reply to you. One of those reasons might include anxiety about not knowing whether any open positions exist at his or her employer. By proactively mentioning the open position you remove any anxiety the Booster may feel about having to do detective work on your behalf.

Should I actually *apply* to that posting before I request an informational interview?

No, not unless the posting includes an imminent deadline. I advise my students to try to conduct the informational interview prior to applying, for two important reasons.

First, a great informational interview may make applying online unnecessary—with a Booster taking your back, you'd be amazed at the exceptions that can and will be made. This will save you precious job search time. I recommend not applying online to that posting until the Booster advises you to do so. Although you don't want to be viewed as high maintenance, you also don't want to be lumped in with those who apply for the position in the most anonymous way possible. Hiring managers will almost never disqualify a pre-screened candidate based on a technicality that can be easily corrected, like not yet having an online application. If your Booster tells you that you actually *do* need to fill out an online application at some point, you can be fairly certain that it will be read.

Second, your informational interviewer will likely be able to give you tips about themes or experiences to stress in your application that will maximize your chance of getting noticed. (Ultimately, it'll be your contact's *referral* that gets you noticed, but asking the Booster's advice here builds that individual's willingness to make that referral. It also pays dividends during interviews: once you have an employer's attention, offering some spot-on messaging—the kind only an inside source could know—is a fast route to an offer.)

So why is the third point—putting your connection first—so important?

For the same reason that nearly every pop song plays its chorus or primary "hook" in the first thirty seconds—you need to give the contact a reason to care quickly so he or she will actually pay attention. Identifying your connection to the contact right up front maximizes your chance of getting your message read.

Let's revisit the ways in which we may have found a contact, from page 83:

1. Most recent alumni database
2. Undergraduate alumni database (if different from above)
3. LinkedIn
4. Facebook
5. Fan Mail
6. LinkedIn backsolving
7. Cold calls

Doing this is easy enough when reaching out to an alum from a previous school—simply mention that you're a current student or fellow alum in your first sentence, as in our example. Because these contacts can be reached directly with minimal effort and typically have a high response rate, we will start with them whenever possible.

With a connection found using LinkedIn, it depends on the nature of the contact. If it is a Group contact, it is identical to the alumni scenario—mention the LinkedIn group of which you are both members in your opening sentence. If your contact is a second-degree connection, however (meaning you are both connected to the same person, but not to each other), ask your connection whether he or she would be willing to make an introduction on your behalf. This gives you instant credibility, and it's one less email you have to write.

If your connection is unable or unwilling to make such an introduction, ask whether the connection is willing to check with the target to see whether it's OK for you to reach out to the target directly. You may need to rekindle that relationship with your mutual contact before that person will vouch for you to your target, so this is better form than using LinkedIn's email infrastructure to skip over your mutual contact and reach out to your target directly (particularly when the first thing your target is likely to do in that case—if anything—is ask your mutual acquaintance what that person thinks of you!).

Regardless, once your target is primed for your approach (if possible), mention your mutual contact in your opening sentence.

The fourth option, contacts found via Facebook, is identical to the second-degree connection scenario on LinkedIn. Ask your contact to make the introduction for you, but if that is not feasible, mention your mutual contact in the first sentence of your outreach email to your target contact.

My students consistently remark that writing the first "connection" sentence to a Fan Mail–based contact is surprisingly easy. This ease stems from the fact that there is something organic and genuine to talk about—specifically, the job seeker's interest in learning more about whatever topic the target had been interviewed about. Change the subject line around a little and your outreach email gets even shorter, allowing you to skip the fourth and fifth points of the 5-Point Email altogether:

SUBJECT: Your interview in last month's *Science* magazine

Dear Dr. Johnson,

I'm just completing my biology degree at Case Western Reserve University, and I found your thoughts on the Cleveland Clinic's trial use of nanomachines to address certain forms of cancer in last month's issue of *Science* to be very interesting.

Would you mind discussing your work further with me in a brief phone chat? I had a few follow-up questions, and your insights would be invaluable.

Thank you for your time,

Jennifer Thomas

Finding the article is the hard part in these outreaches. The upside is that once that article is found, the outreach email practically writes itself!

Similarly, the first sentence found using the LinkedIn backsolving is similar to the Fan Mail approach. It is still ultimately a piece of Fan Mail that looks nearly identical in structure to the example just shown, but the method by which you found it has simply been flipped around.

For cold calls via email, you simply skip the connection sentence, because you have no connection. You go directly to the "ask" of whether they're willing to discuss their experiences with you by phone. It's far from an optimal scenario, but Boosters can be surprisingly open—the flattery of asking for someone to share their insights with you alone may be sufficient to earn a response, regardless of your lack of a connection.

What do you mean by the fourth point— "Generalize your interest"?

This advice is designed to inoculate against the scenario in which a particular Booster's own firm may not be hiring, but he may still have many relevant contacts to share or helpful advice to offer. If, however, the focus of your first outreach email is all about jobs at the contact's employer, once again you may get the "We're under a hiring freeze right now, but good luck elsewhere!" response.

By generalizing your interest to include a logical family of similar employers that share certain traits (while still focusing your interest primarily on your target contact's employer), you accomplish two goals. First, Boosters can be assured that your interest in their firm is sincere and logical (in our example, IBM is indeed a technology company that hires marketing MBAs in North Carolina, so your outreach makes sense).

Second, it encourages Boosters at firms that aren't currently hiring to respond. It's counterintuitive, but these are the best Boosters of all. I call them Super-Boosters. If you still want to talk to them even after they tell you there are no openings (thus proving your sincere dedication to the field), and they like you, they can become your fiercest advocates.

Finding a Booster at a hiring target employer helps you with that one firm, but finding a Super-Booster at a nonhiring target can help you with *several* firms instead of just her own. Boosters want to help, and if their firm is not an option, they may open up their network at multiple other firms to job seekers they like in an incredible fashion. I've seen a number of my students taken under such Boosters' wings, and those lucky few usually end up with one or more offers from people in that Booster's network—or even the Booster's own firm, once they start hiring again.

Therefore, *never turn down an informational interview because of a hiring freeze!* If the contact still offers to help despite that hiring freeze, the payoff can be significant. By including in your outreach email a general description of your scope (for example, tech companies in North Carolina) rather than mentioning only IBM, you offer Boosters insight into your overall strategy and a sense for how they may be able to assist, turning what might be a depressing response for all parties ("Now's not a great time at IBM") into a positive one ("IBM's not hiring right now, but I can point you to a few firms in the area that I know are"). Everyone wins.

Regarding the fifth point, "Maintain control of follow-up"—won't some recruiters see that as presumptuous or threatening?

Regardless of what you write, some contacts will always take offense—it could be your tone, your timing, your font choice—basically, anything. This reaction thankfully tends to be a near-exclusive Curmudgeon/Obligate trait, however! If a contact is that easily offended by an informational interview request, he or she is unlikely to be the kind of Booster you need who will advocate for you to get an interview slot when one opens up. Good riddance, I say!

When you close your 5-Point Emails to Boosters by saying something like "I recognize this may be a busy time for you, so if we are unable to connect by email I'll try to reach you next week to see if that is more convenient," you demonstrate several key desirable traits.

First, you demonstrate deference to their schedules, showing you appreciate that their time is more valuable than yours. The job seeker is the one requesting the favor, so it should be the job seeker's responsibility to revive the outreach if it doesn't work out the first time. Clarifying your ownership of any inconvenience is an elegant way to keep your foot in the door in case your contact doesn't respond immediately.

Second, you demonstrate a commitment to making the connection happen, which differentiates you from the vast majority of job seekers who will email once and give up if they don't hear back. I myself am an Obligate (which many people find surprising, given my career choice!). I typically respond to job seekers only on their second try to get an informational interview with me; those job seekers have demonstrated both resilience and organization—two traits that I value highly.

Third, adding this clause gives a sense of urgency about responding to you, ultimately increasing your response rate (because it has a deadline and is thus less likely to get lost in a contact's inbox). The wording of your follow-up statement should be vague enough to allow you to choose whether to follow-up via phone or email. Some contacts have strong preferences for email versus telephone outreach. Those who prefer email (whom I consider the vast majority) are motivated to respond to you within the week to avoid an interruptive call.

Fourth, and most important, maintaining control of the follow-up allows you to systematically initiate and track your outreach with little to no decision anxiety. In the next chapter, we will discuss how to systematically manage outreach emails to be as efficient and effective as possible, but the fifth point of the 5-Point Email is what makes systematic, decision-free tracking possible.

How does the 5-Point Email make such "worry-free" outreach tracking possible?

Well, unfortunately no alumni database offers checkboxes in each profile specifying "Booster" or "Curmudgeon—don't bother." Thus we need to find some sort of proxy information that will allow us to approximate quickly whether a target contact is a Booster who's likely worth our time or an Obligate or Curmudgeon who's likely not. That proxy information will be our contact's responsiveness—more specifically, the amount of time it takes him or her to respond to our 5-Point Email. We'll cover this specific topic in our next chapter, Track.

If I can't identify Boosters up front, then how do I decide who to send these 5-Point Emails to in the first place?

Great question. Glance again at our hierarchy of contacts on page 83. We went to target contacts with the highest average rate of return on effort first. That is why I had you stop once you found a contact at a certain level on the list—there was no need to employ less-efficient techniques.

If you have multiple options within a level of that hierarchy—for example, if you have twenty different alumni contacts from your most recent alumni database at your #1 target employer, BiffCo—choose the one whose job is most similar to the one you want (or are applying for). His or her insights and network within the company are likely to be the most relevant.

However, if you are seeking a marketing position, and five of those twenty alumni you found are all in marketing, I would choose someone several years my senior, if possible. They are most likely to *themselves* be hiring managers for people at your level, and thus are preferable.

If your only options are very senior or very junior personnel at the employer, I would try the more senior contacts first since they carry two additional important benefits over junior contacts: first, they may not get contacted very often, because job seekers may find their high position intimidating. Second, senior alumni may be too busy to help you, but they may hand you off to a more junior person (who may or may not be an alum) to answer your questions. Such people will likely be highly motivated to help you to the best of their abilities! Unfortunately, junior alumni don't have people they can hand you off to in quite the same way.

That said, I'd still start with a junior alum who holds a position closer to my interests than a more senior alum in a different area of the company I'm targeting. Those more senior people may still be helpful, even if they are in finance and you are targeting marketing, but they may ask you whether you've already reached out to the junior person who works in marketing—that's an awkward question to answer if you haven't already done so!

Even if I *do* target the right contacts, what if they've already received 5-Point Emails from other job seekers?

I get this question frequently, and first off, let me say I'm flattered you think that this widespread epidemic of 5-Point Emails could one day sweep the job search nation!

Personally, I think this effect will be negligible. Even if the 5-Point Email became a standard taught by schools everywhere, it would still be effective simply because all of its alternatives are awful.

One awful alternative is doing nothing at all. Although this method is popular, a 5-Point Email will always outperform not sending an email in the first place!

The second awful alternative is customizing your email to include more personalized information, like what your background is and how you think you can add value to your target employer. Sound familiar? Yes, the primary alternative to the 5-Point Email is the same old four-hundred-word emails we've been sending for years. The ones that nobody likes. No matter how technology changes in the future, short and generic will always be preferable to long and generic. Not only does the 5-Point Email take less time to write, but it's also way easier to read, especially for your target audience of Boosters, who will ask for more background if they actually want or need it.

The third awful alternative is trying something very creative. Not only is this gimmick time-consuming to devise, but it also may alienate as many recipients as it delights, and Boosters don't need to be delighted in order to respond. They simply need to know you need help, so why risk alienating Boosters?

In other words, there is no reason for creativity when faced with a common problem that already has an effective solution. The 5-Point Email is this effective solution. It is succinct, it appeals correctly to your target audience of Boosters, and it requires minimal thought on your part—all great qualities in stressful situations. Even if others start using this method, it will allow hiring managers to quickly differentiate those candidates who are following a proactive and efficient outreach strategy from those who are not, and I for one would much rather talk to candidates from the former group than those from the latter.

Finally, I personally guarantee that if *too many* people start using the 5-Point Email, there will be a future edition of this book that will address in great detail how to handle that very situation. Until then? I wouldn't worry about it. (Although I truly am flattered . . .)

TROUBLESHOOTING

I've been out of school for a few years, so many of the contacts I found are less experienced than I am. Is the 5-Point Email designed for younger job seekers more so than older ones?

Yes and no. Yes, the examples provided here work best when approaching contacts who are equally or more experienced than you are. However, no, the same general rules of the 5-Point Email apply when approaching less-experienced contacts for assistance.

The key issue to remember is that your contact has no incentive to help you other than philanthropy. Thus Boosters will always be your target, because they are the segment most likely to willingly incur inconvenience to help someone in need. In other words, you need for them to like you enough to want to assist. A common mistake I see experienced job seekers make is trying to impress younger contacts with their relevant experience—this is rather wrong-headed. The informational interview is about the contact, not the job seeker (unless the contact wants it to be)—that personal connection, not their assessment of your qualifications, is what earns their advocacy.

The only minor changes to the outreach format will be an emphasis on learning more about the contact's *experience* rather than *insights*. You'll still be asking the person for advice during the informational interview itself—however, it will be more of the "How can I best navigate your organization?" variety, rather than the "What should I do in my first thirty days to get off to a fast start?" kind. The resulting outreach email will look something like this:

SUBJECT: Fuqua MBA seeking your insight about IBM

Dear Benjamin,

My name is Brett DiCola and I am a fellow Fuqua graduate ('99) who found your information in the Fuqua alumni database. May I have 20 minutes to ask you about your experience with IBM? I have spent the last several years in finance at HP and am now seeking to return to North Carolina to be closer to family.

I recognize this may be a busy time for you, so if we are unable to connect by email I'll try to reach you next week to see if that is more convenient.

Best regards,

Brett

This email still shows deference to the contact's expertise in his employer's inner workings, without taking a deferential approach that may create awkwardness when approaching a junior colleague. However, it is important to recognize that Boosters come in all ages, levels of authority, and functions throughout organizations, so it indeed pays to take a genuine interest in the stories of everyone you approach in this process. In addition, younger people still tend to reflexively defer to older people—in professional settings in particular. Therefore, a junior contact may be even more likely to advocate for you than someone similar to you in age, because it's simply common courtesy.

CHAPTER 7

TRACK

 10 MINUTES

I know I'm supposed to track my outreach, so can I skip this chapter?

Unfortunately, most job seekers I work with know they are *supposed* to track their outreach, but they do so either poorly or not at all. Either way, it's devastating to a job search, and it is shockingly common. Thus the purpose of this chapter is to provide you with a simple yet effective method—which I call the 3B7 Routine—for systematically managing the outreach you initiate.

The most common version of "tracking outreach poorly" I see is a job seeker's use of his target employer spreadsheet to track his outreach. Immediately I know this student hates life every time he opens that document because—if not opened daily—spreadsheets are far better for highlighting what the job seeker has *forgotten* to do than what he needs to do in the next day or two.

This is because *a spreadsheet is not a calendaring tool*! It has no calendar functionality, yet I'm shocked by how many people try to use it as such. Microsoft Outlook or Google Calendar (or other programs) *do* have calendar functionality, but for whatever reason they are rarely used by job seekers for that purpose. I think that may be driven by the natural human desire to have all relevant information in one place, but as much as I love spreadsheets, they make terrible alarm clocks.

The more you rely on your memory to keep track of your to-do items, the more mistakes you will make. Not doing what you say you will is devastating in the job search—if you can't keep your word during the job search process, how can potential Boosters trust you to keep your word that you'll follow up with a contact they offer to put you in touch with?

I once reached out to a colleague in healthcare consulting to see if he'd mind speaking with a high school friend of mine who was considering leaving the medical field after her residency. I got his commitment to talk to her and introduced them via email. And she never followed up.

Although the fault was clearly hers (she'd simply lost interest), nevertheless this mishap reflected poorly on me in my colleague's eyes, because I had vouched for someone who didn't follow through on a commitment. Sure, the impact to me was minor, but I had expended effort on behalf of a friend, and I had only embarrassment to show for it.

I don't know whether you've ever had the pleasure of working with or for someone who *always* does what he says he's going to do. I've been working for many years now, and I can honestly say I can count the number of these people I've worked with on one hand. They are incredible, and I'd bring them in on any venture I pursue in the future simply because they removed stress from my life. If they said it would be done, it would be done—I wouldn't have to check in with them ahead of the deadline to see how things were going or anything. They'd find me if they needed help, and I was in managerial bliss.

This is the sort of behavior all job seekers should demonstrate in the job search—that they are the kind of people who *always* do what they say they will. A good tracking system is essential to creating such an impression.

However, there is a second, very important benefit to having a good tracking system—a system specifically designed to work in tandem with the 2-Hour Job Search process.

What is that second benefit?

A good tracking system relieves stress. A tracking system is necessary for successfully tracking job search efforts, mainly because a stressed-out brain is so *bad* at effective tracking.

Biologically, the brain responds to stress by producing cortisol, one unfortunate side effect of which is memory loss. So the more stressed you are, the more forgetful you become. It doesn't matter whether this stress is due to the job search itself, either—it can occur at work, at home, or in your personal life, yet still will yield the same result.

A job search also takes time, and usually that time comes at the expense of sleep. Exhaustion itself causes stress (and thus cortisol). Many job seekers choose to combat this exhaustion with caffeine, but, sadly, caffeine consumption also prompts the brain to churn out cortisol. (Brains just can't catch a break.) Left unchecked, overindulgence in a cocktail of stress, exhaustion, and caffeine can send job seekers into a cortisol-fueled death spiral.

So, will any tracking system do?

No, not if efficiency is your goal. Although any tracking system is better than *no* tracking system, the tracking system I'm about to teach you was designed specifically to maximize the benefit of adopting the 2-Hour Job Search approach. In particular, this tracking system (the 3B7 Routine) is designed to work seamlessly with the 5-Point Emails we learned to write in chapter 6.

In the 3B7 Routine, you'll be letting a computer (specifically, your email software program's calendar application) do all of your remembering for you, sending you pop-up notices whenever it is time to act. This allows you to blissfully forget about the dozens of things you have to do in the next few weeks and focus instead on just the one or two things that you *must* do today. Better yet, it manages all of this without your having to remember a single thing or even open up your LAMP list!

As mentioned earlier, your LAMP spreadsheet will remain *purely* a strategy document, not a tracking document. You will refer to it only when you have time to initiate outreach to a new employer (and thus need to see who's next on your list) or when you want to add new employers to it.

The 3B7 Routine works so well in tandem with the 2-Hour Job Search because it helps you quickly estimate the customer segment (Curmudgeons, Obligates, or Boosters) of each person you email. It gives you a set of precise rules for your follow-up efforts—specifically when to follow up and how to do so, depending on the customer segment you appear to have contacted.

What exactly is the 3B7 Routine, then?

First off, it is an email tracking *routine*. It is standard and replicable—there is no thought, no decision making, and no anxiety involved. Just simple execution.

The "B" in 3B7 refers to business days—your contacts are unlikely to be at work on weekends, so we put our job search efforts on the same schedule. The "3" and "7" in 3B7 refer to the number of business days we will set reminders for after we send an email to a new contact. Each of those reminders will signal us to perform a different action, depending on the response we have (or haven't) received by that point.

The three-business-day reminder notifies us whether the contact we reached out to is likely to be a Booster. As I joked earlier, unfortunately there is no checkbox in an alumni database where people indicate whether they're Boosters or Curmudgeons! Therefore, we must find proxy information we can use to approximate which contact segment they belong to. The 3B7 Routine allows us to rigorously use a contact's response time as an indicator for his or her segment.

If contacts *ever* respond to our outreach, we can assume (by definition) that they are not a Curmudgeon. They can only be Boosters or Obligates, because Curmudgeons simply never write back under any circumstances. That said, I have seen numerous job seekers waste *weeks* on waiting for a Curmudgeon to reply, when it is simply never going to happen. The 3B7 Routine will help ensure we lose no more than two weeks to any Curmudgeon.

Thankfully, Boosters tend to be responsive. They empathize with the difficulties of being in a job search, so they will do their best to get back to you as soon as possible. Having overseen so many job searches, I've found that a majority of employer contacts whom I would define as Boosters will respond within three business days. Look at it this way—if you make a time-sensitive request, would someone who is genuinely interested in your welfare wait a week to respond to you?

This rule of thumb is by no means perfect, but using the 80-20 Rule we can assume that contacts who get back to us within three business days are likely to be Boosters. At least that will be our temporary assumption until they give us reason to believe otherwise.

If we do not hear back from a contact within three business days, assume you've written to either an Obligate (who often likes to footdrag before responding) or a Curmudgeon (who will never write back under any circumstances). In this case, we will want to initiate outreach to a *second* contact at that same company to see whether he or she might be a Booster instead. This allows us to hedge our bets and maintain progress, given that it is unlikely—not *impossible*, but unlikely—that our first contact, if a Booster, would have taken so long to write back.

The seven-business-day reminder serves as our follow-up reminder. Recall that in our initial 5-Point Email, we maintained control of the follow-up. *This is exactly why we did so.* Now following up on an outreach email becomes the routine fulfillment of a promise you've made, rather than an awkward plea for a response—it's simply much easier to be able to open the follow-up with "Per my previous email, I wanted to try you again this week to see if now is a more convenient time for us to briefly chat" rather than "I wrote you a couple of weeks ago, but perhaps you missed it in the large amount of email I'm sure you receive on a daily basis."

So how do I actually *use* the 3B7 Routine?

It's surprisingly simple—any time you send an email to a new contact, you set reminders in your email service's calendar for three and seven business days later. For example, if we send an email to our best contact at our top target employer, BiffCo, on Monday, March 2, we will set our three-business-day reminder for Thursday, March 5, and our seven-business-day reminder for Wednesday, March 11—seven business days after the original email was sent (but nine calendar days later).

Often the most efficient way to set calendar reminders is to just create an appointment for the first thing in the morning called "3-day reminder: BiffCo." That way, when you first check your computer that morning, a pop-up box should be waiting on the computer's desktop, reminding you that some job search action is necessary that day.

In your calendar, this process will look like this:

SUN	MON	TUE	WED	THU	FRI	SAT
1	2 (Sent email to BiffCo)	3	4	5 7 a.m.— 3-day reminder: BiffCo	6	7
8	9	10	11 7 a.m.— 7-day reminder: BiffCo	12	13	14

So what do I do with these reminders?

Your actions will differ according to how your contacts respond. We'll address our best-case scenario first.

Scenario #1:

First contact responds within three business days

If your initial contact responds to you within three business days, then you have struck gold! This is both the best-case and the easiest-to-track scenario. That person appears to be a Booster, so set up an informational interview with him for a later date—something that fits his schedule if he offers you specific time and date guidance in his reply—and cancel your follow-up reminders. (Don't worry about how to actually conduct those informational interviews just yet—we'll cover that in the next chapter.) If your contact does not offer specific times, reply with a simple email that offers a variety of times you may be open in the next week to discuss, like this:

SUBJECT: RE: Fuqua MBA student seeking your advice

Dear Mr. Jones,

Thank you for your quick response and willingness to chat with me. Over the next week, I am free after 1 p.m. on Monday and Tuesday afternoons as well as all day on Wednesday—will any of those times work for you?

Thank you again,

Javier

When a contact doesn't offer you specific times, you can help her by reducing her own decision anxiety by giving her several options. These Boosters are people too, and too many choices can paralyze them as well.

If your Booster does not constrain your choices of when she is free to speak, do so for her in your reply, as shown in the example. It's not fixing your contacts' choices in stone, but giving them a smaller decision set to work with.

Returning to our BiffCo example, if our first contact gets back to us on Wednesday (before we get our three-day reminder pop-up on Thursday), we simply cancel any follow-up reminders associated with BiffCo that pop up—both the three-day reminder on Thursday, March 5, and the seven-day reminder on Wednesday, March 11. It appears that our first contact may actually be a Booster, given the swift response, so let's get this person on the phone as soon as possible to determine whether this is truly the case.

However, if our three-business-day reminder pops up before we get a response from our initial contact, we are going to hedge our bets, as it appears our initial contact is likely either a Curmudgeon or an Obligate.

HOW DO I HEDGE MY BETS?

As I mentioned earlier, in general I see a 40-percent response rate with 5-Point Emails—thus the other 60 percent of the time you're not going to hear back. What do you do then?

If you're like most job seekers, you wait. And wait. And wait some more.

This is a *very* dangerous time for unsophisticated job seekers—specifically, ones who view contacts as a homogeneous, identical bunch rather than as a grab-bag assortment of Curmudgeons, Obligates, and Boosters. These job seekers *so greatly fear* offending anyone that they'll postpone following up on any unanswered outreach as long as possible—often forever.

Without a formal process in place before starting, it will always seem safer to give contacts one more day in the hope that they'll finally respond than to reach out to them a second time, acknowledging the awkward fact that they didn't respond to your first message. Unsurprisingly, most job seekers choose the "safe" path of waiting, despite its ineffectiveness. However, it comes at a price—decision anxiety.

Choosing not to follow up can itself be an excruciating decision, especially when it is a topic that the job seeker struggles with daily, further taxing the job seeker's decision-making capacity. Worse yet, the job seeker usually knows that following up is the right thing to do, so there's often self-loathing as well as lost time involved in these never-ending one-day extensions. It's truly awful to see and far too common, and usually it brings the job seeker's momentum to a screeching halt.

That is why we have both the 5-Point Email and the 3B7 Routine: the former includes a clause that obligates us to follow up if the contact doesn't respond, and the latter ensures that we do indeed follow up as promised—after seven business days, which is usually expressed more gently as "within the next couple of weeks" in our 5-Point Email.

If we haven't heard back from our first contact before our three-day reminder pops up, it's safer to assume she's an Obligate or a Curmudgeon (and thus not worth our time, nor likely to miss us if we go away) rather than a very busy Booster (which happens, but not that often!). Thus, when our three-day reminder pops up, it's time to initiate outreach with a second contact at the same employer.

This means returning to your alumni database, LinkedIn contacts, and so on to find your *second best* or next most relevant contact at your target employer. You will then send this secondary contact a similar 5-Point Email (remembering to change the addressee's name and any other details to reflect any difference in role, relationship, or rank, of course).

The tracking process is exactly the same for the second contact as for the first. Because this email will be your first outreach to that person, you will once again follow the 3B7 Routine and set reminders for three and seven business days after the date of your outreach, noting this time that the reminders apply to contact #2.

Returning to our reminder calendar (see page 131) for our first BiffCo contact, we now want to add reminders for our second contact at BiffCo, because our first contact appears not to be a Booster. This will make our calendar look more like this (with our previous reminders grayed out):

SUN	MON	TUE	WED	THU	FRI	SAT
1	2	3	4	5 7 a.m.—3-day reminder: BiffCo #1	6	7
	(Sent email to BiffCo #1)			(Sent email to BiffCo #2)		
8	9	10 7 a.m.—3-day reminder: BiffCo #2	11 7 a.m.—7-day reminder: BiffCo #1	12	13	14
15	16 7 a.m.—7-day reminder: BiffCo #2	17	18	19	20	21

IN MY OUTREACH EMAIL TO CONTACT #2, SHOULD I MENTION THAT I ALREADY CONTACTED SOMEONE ELSE?

No, that is not necessary. It may appear as if you are "tattling" on contact #1 if you do, and that is not the sort of first impression you want to give. Simply write the same 5-Point Email to the new contact, making no mention that he is your second choice.

STILL, WON'T THE INITIAL CONTACT BE OFFENDED THAT I CONTACTED SOMEONE ELSE?

No. In fact, you'll be doing her a favor.

Curmudgeons *certainly* don't mind if you reach out to someone else, because they were never going to write you back anyway. Obligates might weakly pretend to mind, but in reality they will be relieved that someone else who cares more about your welfare has stepped in. Boosters are the only audience that could possibly mind. However, if you've given them a few days to respond, and then reach out to one more person, your additional effort reflects positively rather than negatively on you, the job seeker.

If you've heard horror stories about employers rejecting candidates who contacted multiple employees at one time, it is because the candidate contacted *many* people simultaneously (think five to ten employees) requesting informational interviews. This is not only a bad use of the job seeker's time (too many similar conversations at one employer), but it also demonstrates a lack of respect on the job seeker's part for that firm's need for actual productivity from its employees.

The crucial difference between the 3B7 Routine and the horror story is that the former uses a serial process appropriately, whereas the latter uses a parallel process inappropriately.

WHAT ARE SERIAL AND PARALLEL PROCESSES?

A serial process is a linear sequence of events. Imagine going through the drive-through at a fast-food restaurant where there are multiple stops. At the first stop, the giant menu with the intercom, you place your order. Then you pull around to the first window, where you pay for your order. Then you pull forward to the second window, where you pick up your food, and finally you drive away. This is a serial process—one step at a time.

Serial processes are good at controlling volume—for example, the fast-food restaurant has only a limited number of cooks, so the number of orders they can handle per hour is limited. Therefore, it would be a bad idea to open more stations where customers could place an order, because the cooks are the bottleneck in the process, resulting in even longer wait times for those who have placed orders.

A parallel process is one in which certain steps are done simultaneously. Think of going to the supermarket and seeing many lanes open through which you can check out—that is a parallel process. (If the store had only one cash register, however, it would become a serial process. Similarly, once you choose a lane, checking out itself becomes a serial process.) If the supermarket is very busy, the store may move personnel away from stocking shelves to operate the checkout lanes, reducing the amount of time people must wait before they can purchase their goods and go home.

Parallel processes are good at being fast and flexible. If a certain step in a process is slow, devoting more people to that step will speed up the entire process. In this job-search process, the slow step is waiting for people to get back to you.

The horror story situation I mentioned earlier is sadly a true one. A former student of mine emailed nearly ten bankers at his top choice firm simultaneously (or "in parallel") to request informational interviews. These bankers sat right next to each other, so they quickly realized they had been spammed by a job seeker, and this student's overzealous outreach quickly became the subject of ridicule.

A parallel process is indeed the fastest way for this student to find a contact. It would always be the correct approach if none of the contacts could communicate with each other and the student had an infinite amount of time to conduct informational interviews with anyone who said "yes." Unfortunately, just like the Disney ride says, "It's a small world, after all," and none of us has infinite time.

A serial process, although slower, is more appropriate for job search outreach—at least initially. The 3B7 Routine represents a serial/parallel hybrid: you start with one contact at a time (serially), but if she doesn't get back to you within three business days, you reach out to a secondary contact in parallel. This doubles your chance of finding a Booster at a target employer quickly without risking alienating the organization along the way. (And of course, you'll be reaching out to several *employers* in parallel at one time as well.)

Ideally, the first Booster you find at the firm will be able to play "traffic cop" and point you to the best person to talk to next. Large employers in particular often have a team captain for each school from which they hire who is responsible for screening potential hires. If that's the case, it's nice to find that out within just one informational interview instead of two or more, when possible. Thus, not only does a serial/parallel hybrid approach project professionalism, but it also saves you time.

BACK TO THE BIFFCO EXAMPLE: WHAT IF I DON'T HEAR FROM THE FIRST *OR* SECOND CONTACT?

The 3B7 Routine is so effective because it lets you know whether *two* people are likely to be Boosters before you have to follow up with either one of them. This leads us to Scenarios #2 and #3. Scenario #2 tells you what to do when your second contact appears to be a Booster and responds quickly; Scenario #3 tells you what to do when *neither* your first nor your second contact gets back to you before you get your first seven-day reminder for that target employer.

Scenario #2:

First contact doesn't respond within three business days; second contact does

Look back at our updated calendar for after we reach out to a second contact (see page 135); again, the grayed text is from our original calendar and the bolder text shows how we would update our calendar if we *didn't* hear from contact #1 within three business days. Note that we'll receive our three-day reminder for BiffCo contact #2 on Tuesday, March 10—one day before we receive our seven-day reminder for BiffCo contact #1. This is by design.

The action we take when we receive the seven-day reminder for contact #1 depends on how responsive contact #2 was. In this scenario, we'll assume that contact #2 responds within three business days (say on Friday, March 6, or Monday, March 9), indicating the contact may be a Booster, whereas contact #1 remains unresponsive. Obviously, BiffCo contact #2 is the one we want to engage more, given the contact's apparently greater interest in us. However, we *did* obligate ourselves to follow up with contact #1 at the end of our 5-Point Email (see page 110). Therefore, we have to reach out to contact #1 when our seven-day reminder pops up, *even if we've already heard back from contact #2*. That said, in this scenario, in which contact #2 responds quickly whereas contact #1 does not respond at all, we'll follow up by email (not by phone) in the hopes that he'll once again fail to respond, leaving us more time to focus on contact #2.

In this case, in your follow-up you should continue to express interest in speaking with him, but only weakly, as in this example:

SUBJECT: Duke MBA checking in to seek your advice

Dear Contact #1,

I'm sorry we were unable to connect in the last week, and I wanted to see whether this is a better time to talk about your experiences to date at BiffCo.

Please let me know if so, and thank you for your time.

Best regards,

Job Seeker

Short and sweet. Recall, we don't *really* want to hear back from contact #1, because contact #2 has proven to be more responsive and is thus more likely to be a Booster. However, because we did obligate ourselves to follow up, a short email like the example will suffice.

In short, we're trying to let contact #1 down easy without the situation being our fault. It's counterintuitive to spend time on someone you are no longer interested in speaking with, but we want to maintain our reputation for always fulfilling our commitments above all else, even if it means an extra informational interview here or there.

Scenario #3:

Neither contact #1 or #2 responds

Let's take one more look at our example calendar. In this scenario, #3, it's March 10 and we've heard nothing from contact #1 (after six business days) or contact #2 (after three). In this case we'll follow up with contact #1 *by phone* on the following day, Wednesday, March 11—preferably early in the day during business hours, because this time we *do* want a response. Time is a precious commodity we can't afford to waste.

SUN	MON	TUE	WED	THU	FRI	SAT
1	2 (Sent email to BiffCo #1)	3	4	5 7 a.m.— 3-day reminder: BiffCo #1 (Sent email to BiffCo #2)	6	7
8	9	10 7 a.m.— 3-day reminder: BiffCo #2	11 7 a.m.— 7-day reminder: BiffCo #1	12	13	14
15	16 7 a.m.— 7-day reminder: BiffCo #2	17	18	19	20	21

There are two key benefits to conducting this follow-up by phone. First, it demonstrates a pattern of escalating interest. A person who gets overwhelmed by email may be more likely to respond to a phone call or voice mail message, and because we don't have an unlimited amount of time to wait to find a "foothold" contact to help get us started, we'd rather hear back from an Obligate now than take several additional weeks to find a Booster (whom the Obligate may be able to point you toward directly).

Second, the phone call follow-up is actually faster to make than a follow-up email is to write. Tone and intent are sometimes misconstrued in an email, but are much less likely to be confused on a voice message. My rule is to always switch from email to the phone whenever things stop going according to plan. There is no need to leave detailed messages, either. Just ask for the contact to give you a call back at his convenience, or read out loud whatever your follow-up email would have said; for example:

Hello, Contact #1. This is Job Seeker, and my phone number is 555-555-5555. Per my previous email, I wanted to follow up to see whether this might be a better week for a brief phone conversation. I'd really appreciate the chance to ask you some questions about your experience at BiffCo. Once again, my number is 555-555-5555, and I look forward to hearing back from you.

Phone calls are harder to ignore because they are interruptive (the ring itself distracts the recipient from his current task) and are harder to "lose" in an email inbox. Furthermore, they leave a less conspicuous paper trail. This is an especially key point for job seekers working in a second language. There are no spelling mistakes in conversation, and grammatical errors are far less noticeable when spoken than when written down. Plus, voice messages are faster to prepare than error-free emails.

After making that follow-up call, we put one last reminder into our calendar, a ten-day reminder (ten business days from the first contact, but three business days from our telephone call). Consider this our "backstop." See the calendar for how this looks in practice (with new entries in bold):

SUN	MON	TUE	WED	THU	FRI	SAT
1	2 [Sent email to BiffCo #1]	3	4	5 7 a.m.—3-day reminder: BiffCo #1 **[Sent email to BiffCo #2]**	6	7
8	9	10 **7 a.m.—3-day reminder: BiffCo #2**	11 7 a.m.—7-day reminder: BiffCo #1 **Call BiffCo #1 to follow up**	12	13	14
15	16 **7 a.m.—7-day reminder: BiffCo #2** **10-day reminder: BiffCo #1**	17	18	19 **10-day reminder: BiffCo #2** **[Send email to BiffCo #3]**	20	21

If a contact has not responded to an email for seven business days, nor a follow-up phone call for three business days, what more can you realistically do? The person is likely a Curmudgeon and will never respond. It's the Curmudgeon's loss, I say.

Notice, too, that the ten-day reminder coincides with the seven-day reminder for contact #2. Again, this is not by accident. On Monday, March 16, we know contact #1 is unlikely to ever get back to us, so it's time to call contact #2 in a similar fashion and set a second ten-day reminder.

On Thursday, March 19, if neither of our contacts has gotten back to us after an initial email and a follow-up call, we essentially reboot the process: we email BiffCo contact #3 and set three-day and seven-day reminders, just as we did for BiffCo contact #1.

Once you get started with the 3B7 Routine, there's really no decision making, thought work, or anxiety; you're just executing a plan (albeit one with unpredictable results) over and over until you get the desired outcome (that is, a response from a Booster).

What if I get the contact live on the phone during my follow-up call?

This is great news! Ask her if you can take a couple of minutes of her time to schedule an informational interview with her for the next week or so. This way, you are minimally interrupting what is already likely a fully booked day for this Booster.

What if the Booster says, "Now is a good time to talk—what questions do you have for me?"

In that case, you go ahead with the informational interview. Especially because the person didn't respond to your first outreach, if it turns out that he's an Obligate, you want to know that sooner rather than later, so you can return to the process of identifying a Booster at your target employer.

This is typical—though not universal—Obligate behavior; the Obligate is looking to get this conversation over with, and hoping to keep it short by keeping it an "unscheduled" event. However, that doesn't necessarily mean this conversation won't be helpful.

Don't worry about getting caught on the spot during a phone call follow-up. In chapter 9, you will learn a structure called the TIARA Framework that I developed for leading effective informational interviews—even in cases when you've had little to no time to prepare. With this in your toolbox, you'll know *exactly* how to handle such situations!

The three examples we've just walked through cover the vast majority of the scenarios you'll encounter. Most contacts who respond will do so within three business days of either your initial outreach or your seven-business-day follow-up, and those who haven't responded by then almost certainly never will. However, there are exceptions.

Scenario #4:

Exceptions to Scenarios #1, #2, and #3

Occasionally, contacts will get back to you at odd intervals. The two primary odd intervals are: (1) between three to seven business days after your first or second outreach, and (2) long after your follow-up outreach (weeks or months later).

For the first group, contacts that respond to you after the three-business-day cutoff, you are still obligated to conduct an informational interview with them if they are willing. Granted, you may have already heard back from contact #2, who could be a Super-Booster, but an extra informational interview isn't the worst thing that can happen in the job search.

If you haven't heard from contact #2 by the time contact #1 reaches out (belatedly), then of course schedule an informational interview with contact #1. A response more than three business days after you sent it does not mean *definitively* that your contact is not a Booster. It just means it is less likely.

For the second group—contacts responding to you weeks or even months later—assuming you have found better options by then, thank them for their response, update them on your progress, and wish them a nice day. You have no reason to feel bad in this case—just as nobody would hire a plumber or mechanic who waited weeks to return a call. No job seeker should rely upon contacts who behave similarly.

Should I ever reach out to a third contact while the first two are still in process?

You can, but I recommend experimenting with this only after you've got some 3B7 Routine experience under your belt. Although we are focusing only on BiffCo in this illustration, we are going to be reaching out to multiple employers at one time in the same fashion.

Once job seekers get more comfortable with the 3B7 Routine, I tell them to reach out to a third contact only for time-sensitive opportunities (ones with active job postings, or if a job acceptance due date is pending) or when they are certain that they'll be able to reply to all potential responses within one business day. Depending on the urgency and the job seeker's bandwidth, the right time to initiate outreach to BiffCo contact #3 in our example is Monday, March 16 (by this time we know with relative certainty that contact #1 is a Curmudgeon).

Note: For time-*critical* situations, job seekers can reach out to contact #3 as early as Tuesday, March 10, when the three-day reminder pops up for contact #2 (assuming neither contact #1 nor contact #2 has responded by then), because it appears that neither of the previous contacts is a Booster. However, it does complicate tracking significantly to have three people active at once, and you can end up having to do up to three informational interviews with Obligates who respond to your second outreach but not your first. Thus, initiating that third contact may increase the speed with which you finally connect, but it may cost you time in the long run. If that trade-off is acceptable and you are confident your follow-up quality will not suffer because of it, I wholeheartedly support such an approach when necessary!

So I understand the 3B7 Routine for BiffCo. What do I do with my other top target employers?

The exact same thing. Although I advocate using a (primarily) *serial* process for each particular employer, I advocate using a *parallel* process across many employers. Thus, you'll be conducting the 3B7 Routine for many employers at the same time.

How many employers should I contact at one time?

Only five, at least to start with—that's what the ten-minute dura-tion specified at the start of this chapter assumes, at least. Because the typical hit rate on 5-Point Emails is about 40 percent, that means you should hear back from two of the first five contacts you reach out to within three business days. This allows you to get a couple of informational interviews scheduled and underway while you wait for the reminders to pop up for the others, signaling you to take further actions.

As you become more comfortable with the 3B7 Routine, you can increase the number of employers you engage at one time to ten or more if your time allows, but it's important to remember that per-fect execution is more important than contacting more employers faster—in the latter case, you risk spreading yourself too thin, and a slow response to a Booster who is offering you open times for an informational interview is one of the two quickest ways to lose that Booster. (We'll address the second way to quickly lose a Booster in chapter 8, on informational interviewing.)

TROUBLESHOOTING

What if I only have *one* contact at an employer in my alumni database, and he doesn't respond to me within three business days?

There will be cases where you don't have a second contact ready and available at an employer, and your first contact appears not to be a Booster. In this case, don't panic. Procrastination in this situation is actually a good thing. There is still a chance that contact #1 could be a Booster, saving you the effort of ever having to track down a contact #2. However, if the three-day reminder pops up without a response from contact #1, that's the time to resume working your way down the contact hierarchy (see page 83) to find a suitable contact #2.

The bottleneck (or speed-limiting step) in the outreach process is the waiting for people to get back to you. This dead time is useful for finding replacement contacts when your previous ones don't pan out.

Do I really need to follow up with contact #1 if he or she doesn't respond but contact #2 does?

Yes, absolutely. You gave your word, and keeping it is one of the few demonstrations of competence you can *prove* prior to interviewing for a job. Contact #1 may know that contact #2 has responded to you by the time you follow up and thus may ignore that as well; however, your conscientiousness will have left an indelible impression.

Furthermore, having *none* of this process be optional—which means there is no question that you will follow up with contact #1—actually saves you both time and anxiety. It's far quicker to crank out an obligatory follow-up email than it is to think about whether or not it is worth your time, especially when contact #2 is more responsive than contact #1 and your seven-day follow-up email is a writing task you'll need to accomplish only once, after which you can easily modify it to send out again.

In short, optional activities are harder to do than mandatory ones. Think of following up on unresponsive contacts in the job search as like flossing your teeth as a child (or in my case, as a grown-up)—it's not for you to *like*, it's for you to *do*.

Step 2 Wrap-Up

Launching Step 2 with a plan in place is critical, because getting back to potential Boosters within twenty-four hours is absolutely essential. Setting reminders several days out each time you send an email may feel odd, especially given that the person may write you right back within minutes. However, *it allows you to temporarily forget those who are slow to respond* while focusing on those who give you their attention—a much healthier perspective to keep throughout this process.

I often see my students fall weeks behind on sending thank-you emails to the employer contacts they've spoken to—they simply become busy with other things, and then they'll ask me, "Is three days/three weeks/three months too long to wait to send a thank-you email?"

Thank-you notes are electronic receipts that you spoke to someone. I have an awful memory, so at my previous jobs I had an email folder called "Thank-yous" where I'd file any thank-you note I got to help me remember whom I spoke to, knowing that my memory inevitably would fail me. We'll revisit this in the final chapter on following up (chapter 10), but there is an important parallel here.

All the hard work you put in during the outreach process can be squandered *very* quickly if you don't respond right away to the people who are trying to help you. Don't fixate on those who haven't responded yet; let your reminders guide you through managing those contacts, while you spend your time focusing on those who are most likely to help you find jobs.

You've done great work up to this point. Just remember to give your best customers (Boosters who respond to you quickly) the white-glove treatment. The rest will get their follow-ups in time, but remember that the goal of the Contact step is finding Boosters. Responding to *incoming* job search email takes priority over initiating outgoing emails, because incoming emails from employers mean they have already taken an interest in you. Follow-up emails to unresponsive contacts can be a day or too late if need be, but sending response emails to the Boosters you hear back from should *never* take longer than twenty-four hours!

RECRUIT:
Informational
Interviewing

CHAPTER 8

RESEARCH

15 MINUTES PER INTERVIEW

I know I'm supposed to research employers, but how much research is enough?

Research is like learning or practicing—there's no explicit finish line or ending point, which indeed makes this advice rather maddening to receive. The purpose of this chapter isn't to teach you how to research for term papers, investments, or even actual job interviews (though it will have some parallels to that last one).

No, the purpose of this chapter is to teach you how to research for informational interviews as efficiently as possible. For informational interviews, there is a lot that *could* be researched, but only a few key items that absolutely *must* be—separating the wheat from the chaff first involves understanding what informational interviews are.

So what exactly *is* an informational interview?

An informational interview is a conversation between an information seeker (nearly always a job hunter) and an information keeper (usually, but not always, an employee at one of the job seeker's target employers). The information seeker then leads the conversation to collect relevant information about the information keeper's career and her path to her current employer.

This concept was first coined back in 1970 by Richard Bolles in the job search blockbuster *What Color Is Your Parachute?*, and it still has not gone out of style. In fact, it is more important now than ever before, because these days no hiring manager has time to genuinely consider every resume that gets submitted to each online job posting. That said, the act of conducting an informational interview used to itself be sufficient for advancing you in the process. Today, informational interviews must be pursued, used, and leveraged properly in order to land an actual job interview, so we'll break down Step 3 as follows:

	TIME REQUIRED
Chapter 8: Research	15 minutes
Chapter 9: Discuss	30 minutes
Chapter 10: Follow-Up	Ongoing
Total for Step 3	45 minutes per interview

In the Internet era, the focus of an informational interview is two-fold: first, to build rapport, and second, to gain usable information. Of the two, building rapport is more important, because if rapport is established, then usable information can be collected at a later date. However, the reverse is not always true. Therefore, the primary focus should be on connecting with your interviewer, and the secondary focus should be collecting information that will help you later in interviews, cover letters, and subsequent informational interviews (or "informationals" for short).

Why should I bother with informational interviews when I could be applying to job postings directly instead?

If the job search were logical and fair, job postings would *absolutely* be a more direct route to employment than informational interviewing. However, the job search is *not* fair. These days the job seeker with the best advocacy network—not the one with the best experience—gets the job.

Recall that hiring managers get hundreds of resumes overnight for any jobs they post online—too many for them to review, especially when they have projects they have to complete to keep their jobs—projects that do *not* include finding the perfect candidate for their current opening. Finding a safe, "good enough" candidate quickly is far preferred.

Therefore, informationals are an absolutely necessary step to getting onto a target employer's internal referral "call list" when an opening arises. You'll be a known quantity who clearly cares enough about the job to make the effort to establish contact, rather than just a nameless person who emails a resume their way.

Though this approach seems indirect to you as a job seeker, it is quite direct for a hiring manager. Why comb through hundreds of candidates when you can start with five to ten preapproved ones first?

So I found a Booster who's willing to do an informational with me—what do I talk to him about?

First off, great job. The goal of this process is to get potential Boosters on the phone to gain their trust, so mission accomplished! There will be many to follow, and soon you will see that they are nothing to be scared of. Furthermore, your performance in them dramatically improves even after just one or two iterations.

Informationals are a bit hard to visualize before you actually conduct your first one. In the TIARA Framework, I split informational interviews into three specific phases:

1. Small talk

2. Questions and answers

3. Next steps

We'll cover each of these three phases in more detail in the next chapter, but knowing the structure of the conversation will help you identify research that will help you achieve your dual goals of building rapport and gaining usable information. A majority of the benefit of the research you learn to conduct in this chapter will pay off during the conversation's second phase, Questions and Answers (Q&A).

Please tell me that by "research" you don't mean "learn everything I can about the employer"?

Oh dear. If you've gotten advice like this in the past, I'm sorry. It's the worst kind of advice—both too easy to give and impossible to follow, serving more to stress you out than to actually assist you.

Obviously, it's impossible (and inefficient) to learn *everything* about an employer before an informational. Research prior to an informational is indeed critical, but once again the 80-20 Rule applies. Some pieces of information are far more important than others, so we'll gather 80 percent of *that* information in a fraction of the time it would take to become an "expert" on a particular employer or industry, especially given that the person you'll be speaking to will be far more knowledgeable than you, no matter how much you prepare!

Your contact should be your ultimate source of information—you simply want to gather enough knowledge ahead of time in order to demonstrate proper respect for the contact's time and to be conversant on any current topics the employer may bring up. In this chapter, I'll teach you how to do this with no more than fifteen minutes of effort.

Remember that your dual goal in this conversation is to build rapport and gain usable information. The focus of this conversation should be entirely on your contact, not on you. A selfless informational interviewer is the best informational interviewer. Why? Because selfless informational interviewers spend the most time getting to know their contacts, which reassures them that you'll likely do the same with anyone (especially more senior people) they pass you on to later, ensuring that their professional reputation is protected.

You do not have an infinite amount of time to conduct research on your employers prior to an informational interviewer, however. In fact, you may recall how strenuously I've advised you *against* research earlier in this process because of its poor return on effort prior to having an informational interview scheduled with an employer. Once that conversation is scheduled, *then* it is time to conduct more in-depth research.

What research do I need to collect in order to reap 80 percent of the benefit in 20 percent of the time?

The research will consist of two parts—external preparation and internal preparation. The external preparation, or information about the company, should take only about fifteen minutes, and its main purpose is to get you conversant on issues likely to be at the top of the mind of the employee you'll be speaking to. The internal preparation, or readiness for questions your informational interviewer is likely to ask *you*, may take longer depending on how much interview practice you've had to date.

What external preparation do I need to do?

At a minimum, you should check three references prior to any informational interview:

1. DataMonitor360 SWOT analysis (if available)
2. Headlines on the front page of the employer's website
3. Google recent employer headlines (and informational interviewers themselves)

DataMonitor360 is an online database that provides SWOT analyses (brief overviews summarizing the Strengths, Weaknesses, Opportunities, and Threats facing a particular employer) for most major public companies. This website does require a subscription, which if you're a student your school is likely to have already. If you are no longer a student, you should be able to access it via your local library.

This is not necessary, nor is it available for every employer you are targeting (the smaller the organization is, the less likely it is available). If it is, however, it is quite simply the best five minutes of research you can do on any employer, because it summarizes the macro trends most impacting them in a very concise format. I made it all the way through several recruiting seasons at business school using *only* SWOT analyses from DataMonitor360 (then called MarketLine), so these are especially dear to me. If you lack access to these reports, "insider guides" like those provided by companies like Vault and WetFeet may also give you information in a similar format about certain well-known firms.

However, Google is always an option as well, and one that takes even less time than the first two resources. Just Googling the company's name and "trends" will give you a good approximation of what that employer is facing right now, if not directly lead you to the company's annual report or Form 10-K, in which the CEO summarizes the "state of the union" for the firm.

These days most employers—those who regularly update their websites, at least—tend to put up their positive headlines on the front page of their website. That is why I recommend looking there next. You want to make sure you're aware of any recent product launches, new facility openings, or promotional campaigns. Several times I've heard nightmare stories from students who went confidently into an informational interview, only to immediately be stumped by the question "Did you see our big headline this week?" *That's* a bad start. The good news is that employers tend to make their good news very easy to find on their website. Then you can at least mention something positive the employer announced recently. Even if it's not the specific headline your interviewer wanted to speak about.

Finally, on the flip side, you'll want to Google headlines about this prospective employer to make sure you're aware of any problem areas the employer is facing right now, such as recent layoffs, turmoil in leadership, or product failures. Although raising such issues demonstrates that you have done some research on the employer, it puts the interviewer in an uncomfortable position: she may feel pressured to speak negatively about her company. This awkwardness will (rightly) be attributed to you, the job seeker, for asking the embarrassing question, which will lead her to believe you might do the same if she were to refer you to a colleague of hers for another informational. Therefore, the point of checking for any major *negative* news about the company is to be prepared to steer clear of it. An ounce of prevention . . .

If you see no negative headlines, then I recommend revising your search to focus on any interesting recent headlines in major publications. I recommend limiting the results of your Google search to only those headlines posted within the past year.

Before you leave Google, search on your informational interviewer's name and company and see what information is publicly available. This is just good due process, potentially giving you an overview of his career history on LinkedIn, for example, or some sense for his activities outside of work you may be able to use as an icebreaker.

Should I mention that I Googled my interviewer before our conversation, or does that risk making me look like a stalker?

It depends on *what* information you plan to reveal that you found while Googling your employer! Some of it is totally appropriate to mention directly, some of it is not. Information that is fair game to mention in an informational interview includes:

- LinkedIn profile information (if you have access to the contact's profile through a Group or second-degree or better connection)

- Biographical information on the employer's website
- Interviews the contact may have conducted with news organizations, magazines, or industry blogs

Information that you should *not* mention having found via Google includes:

- Personal blog information (unless that blog is primarily professionally focused)
- Nonprofessional media mentions (for example, marriage announcements or marathon race results)
- Facebook information that is open to the public (this is usually accidental; there are still far too many of us who need to tighten our privacy settings)

That said, establishing rapport with your interviewer is critical, and identifying a shared passion is an excellent way to do so. Therefore, let's discuss a strategy for how to gracefully accomplish this when you're unsure of the appropriateness of your potential icebreaker.

Let's say you Google an employee with whom you are about to have an informational interview, and the only result you find is an interview she did with a local newspaper about why she's continued to run marathons for more than twenty years.

This is a great potential route to rapport with your interviewer if you also enjoy distance running. However, bringing up this article is risky. Some interviewers may not mind that you found that article online and brought it up, being very happy to chat at length about a topic so close to their hearts. However, other interviewers may be creeped out that you brought up an obscure article that clearly implies you Google stalked them in order to try to establish rapport. So the potential value of mentioning this article is unclear—it could work for or against you.

Therefore, the ideal strategy is to find a way to broach that topic (a fondness for distance running) without mentioning the article. The best way to do this is to dangle that possible connection out to your contact when you are inevitably asked, "Tell me about yourself."

If you enjoy running, mention it as an addendum to your story, concluding your career path with, "In addition, my hobbies include yoga and training for my first half-marathon." This allows the interviewer a graceful opening to share her own passion for running with you if she so desires.

Remember, your contacts don't want this conversation to be awkward either, so they will seek to find common ground with you early on. Including some personal information in your background story—especially if you have reason to believe they share similar hobbies—is a courtesy to them, offering a topic that both of you can use to break the ice.

They may choose not to, however—not wishing to get personal at all, but preferring to focus on your professional interests. I've had some colleagues who are wonderful people but simply do not like sharing personal information. In this case, it's far better that your mention of hobbies disappears into the ether and the focus shifts back to professional concerns.

Is any more external preparation necessary?

No, that's it, and the best part is that all three of the listed items can be done in fifteen minutes. Spending more time than that can actually backfire.

Job seekers who over-research in advance of informationals tend to come across as know-it-alls or self-centered. Keep in mind that your *best* source of information is the contact who's agreed to speak to you. That said, it is your responsibility to create a list of questions that make wise use of their time—questions that either build rapport or help you acquire usable information (or both). The key is to avoid asking them anything you can find on the Internet, and that's why the TIARA Framework is such a helpful guide. Before we discuss that, however, we need to discuss *internal preparation*.

What internal preparation do I need to do for informational interviews?

Informationals usually start off with easy small talk, but you'll need to be prepared to answer the Big Three—three questions so frequently asked during any interview (informational or otherwise) that they get their own nickname.

Even though in the introduction I explicitly said that this is not a book about interviewing, given how commonly the Big Three appear during informationals, job seekers *must* be prepared for them. Therefore, I will address just these three questions, because you often must navigate them effectively during an informational in order to get that first "formal" interview. Here are the Big Three:

1. Tell me about yourself (also known as "Walk me through your resume").

2. Why do you want to work for our organization?

3. Why do you want to work in this industry (say, energy)/ function (say, marketing)?

The Big Three give interviewers a few measures with which they can compare you, apples-to-apples, with other job search candidates. Interviewers find it incredibly hard to compare one person's advertising accomplishments, for example, to another person's journalism or engineering accomplishments.

Thus interviewers, seeking to be fair, are likely to assume that all candidates' accomplishments are roughly equivalent—they all made it to the interview, right? This assumption frees them from a lot of decision anxiety and allows them to focus on presentation and content, which they are better able (and thus prefer) to judge.

If this behavior sounds familiar, it should. It is the same rationalizing logic a hiring manager would use to ignore the hundreds of resumes received online for an open position—it would be unfair to look at only some of them, and there's not enough time to review them all.

However, the Big Three questions elicit candidate answers that *can* be directly compared. There is nothing engineering- or journalism-specific about why a candidate wants now to work in marketing, for example. The credibility of these three answers is therefore especially important, because poor performance here may encourage lazier interviewers to rule you out right away, saving their energy for candidates able to effectively answer these three very fair and fundamental questions.

So how do I answer the Big Three?

The first one—"Tell me about yourself"—is the most common for informational interviews. The recruiter's goal here is to form rapport with you and simultaneously try to assess why your interest in her organization today *makes sense*. The maximum duration of this story (and of all of your interview answers, in fact) should be two minutes. Packing your life story into two minutes is impossible, but it's entirely feasible if you focus on the transitions of your life—which are the parts the recruiter cares about—rather than the "normal time."

A great framework that will keep you on track for this question is, "First, I pursued hypothesis A. What I liked about that decision was B. What I wanted to change was C, leading me to pursue new hypothesis D." So be sure to tell your story in chronological order—it is far easier for an interviewer to follow your logic moving forward than backward. Here is an example of this approach in action:

> I chose to start my career in strategy consulting out of college so I could apply my creativity and logic skills on a variety of different projects. I loved working with clients to help them meet their needs, both spoken and unspoken. However, I missed having any actual final decision-making authority—that was always up to the client.
>
> Thus, I thought marketing would be a great next step—I could maintain the creativity of my work and my enjoyment of

understanding consumers' needs, but I would then get to "pull the trigger" on a plan as well. That is why I joined my current marketing employer three years ago.

Where you start your story depends on your experience level: undergraduates can start with high school or college interests, graduate-level job seekers can start with college or their first job out of college, and more experienced hires can start later than that.

The key point is that *this is your life story.* Enjoy telling it. Really, how often do you get to talk for two minutes uninterrupted these days? Make it engaging, logical, and easy to follow, and don't be afraid to admit mistakes in your hypotheses along the way. In interviews, I appreciate when candidates acknowledge mistakes in their past—it makes me confident they will disclose any future mistakes they may make on the job and suggests an openness to taking feedback, because they know they aren't perfect.

Finally, be prepared to mention any particularly unique or important hobbies or community involvements. Remember, the primary goal of this interview is to form rapport. If asking your interviewer questions during the small-talk phase doesn't naturally result in rapport development, disclosing personal information in the hopes that your interviewer will reciprocate is another way to possibly kick-start a connection.

What about the other two of the Big Three?

"Why are you interested in our organization?" and "Why are you interested in our function/industry?" are less common in informational interviews, but they do appear. Ideally, what you learn in the informational interview will make these questions much, much easier to answer in an actual interview for two main reasons: first, you are getting insider information rather than information from the Internet, and second (and more important), you can *source* your assertions.

If a tech company has a reputation for a work-hard, play-hard environment, it's one thing to say, "I want to work for your tech company because of its work-hard, play-hard culture." That may be true, but you may get a follow-up question like, "How do you know that's true?" If you're relying on rumors or Internet sources, your weak research will be noted.

Ideally, you'll have done an informational interview in advance of your *actual* interview, so your answer can become, "I spoke to your product manager, Catherine Kelly, a couple of weeks ago. I asked her what her favorite part of working for your firm was, and she mentioned how much she enjoyed the firm's 'work-hard, play-hard' environment. That really resonated with me." Your interviewer may disagree with the work-hard, play-hard sentiment, but he won't actually be disagreeing *with you*. He can take that disagreement up with Catherine Kelly, but you did your due process and managed to cite an informational interview you did along the way.

A good template to follow for these questions is assertion-proof-tieback for up to three points that you want to highlight during your two-minute answer.

For example, if asked why high-tech appeals to you as an industry:

There are three main reasons I'm drawn to high-tech: my love of gadgets, the speed of innovation, and making products that improve people's lives.

ASSERTION: *I have been fascinated by new technologies ever since I was a child.*

PROOF: *I still remember the first time I read about Moore's Law—the rule of thumb that says processing speed will double every two years—and I'm stunned at how true it's been. I read* Slashdot *and* Boing Boing *daily to keep up-to-date on the industry, and even after all these years the industry still fascinates me.*

TIEBACK: *My passion for the industry and my constant consumption of news about it from a variety of sources gives me confidence I can quickly gain expertise on any product I might manage in the future.*

The tieback is usually not appropriate to actually state up front in an informational—it may be viewed as overly aggressive or too great a "hard sell," given that your conversation is ostensibly about information and advice rather than jobs. However, having a tieback prepared is important, because many contacts will follow up with a question like "How do you think your passion for technology might help you as a product manager?" to gauge your thoughtfulness. In those cases, it's always good to have tiebacks ready and to make assertions that you're particularly well qualified for!

Is that really all the preparation I need to do for an informational interview?

Obviously, you can research an employer forever, but doing more than necessary is an inefficient use of time. You hit the point of diminishing returns quickly. You are looking for lively conversation topics during your research, not complex "stump your contact" questions. Contacts at your target employers are people too, so they also become uncomfortable when asked questions they don't have answers to. These contacts will then associate feeling embarrassed with talking to you, which makes them less likely to recommend you to someone else out of concern that you'll similarly embarrass their colleague.

As you'll see in the next chapter, the questioning algorithm in the TIARA Framework is designed to *never* stump your contact—most of the questions can be answered (with valuable information) just as well by a first-year analyst as by a thirty-year veteran of an organization. Plus, they tend to be fun and engaging questions to answer in general.

So if I'm prepared for the Big Three, doing only fifteen minutes of research for an informational interview is OK?

Absolutely—as long as it's the *right* fifteen minutes of research!

What if I'm interested in investment banking? I've heard sometimes informationals can become actual interviews without notice.

That is the one glaring exception to the above advice. For investment banking (IB), this can and does commonly happen. Certain contacts simply prefer to spend that time actually interviewing you—complete with questions about the stock market's performance that day, several stocks you'd recommend right now, and so on—rather than allowing you to ask them questions.

When pursuing a career in investment banking, prepare for informational interviews as described in this chapter, but also be prepared for that informational to turn into a real interview. Invest in a good investment banking interviewing book, and study that as well.

Thankfully, IB is the exception rather than the rule in this respect. Few if any other industries act in a similar fashion. In these other industries, you will be allowed (and expected) to lead the conversation.

TROUBLESHOOTING

What if I can't find much information about one of my targets because it is very small and/or privately held?

Again, your best source of information about an organization is the actual informational interviewer. As long as you spend the fifteen minutes trying to complete the external preparation recommended earlier, you have done your due diligence. This story may even prove to be an effective icebreaker, letting your contacts know how their insights are *especially* appreciated, given how little you were able to uncover during your research for this conversation. There are secretive companies out there, so the fact that you know their employer falls into this category is itself an insight.

## CHAPTER 9

DISCUSS

I've set up informational interviews with several Boosters—now what am I supposed to talk about with them?

Recall from the preceding chapter that the purpose of the informational interview is to both form rapport and gain usable information. The TIARA Framework you're about to learn in this chapter breaks the informational interview into three distinct phases: (1) small talk, (2) questions and answers, and (3) next steps. Before we discuss each of those phases in detail, however, let's take a moment to learn about the *Ben Franklin effect*, otherwise known as "why informational interviews work."

What is the Ben Franklin effect?

It is a psychology concept related to the "foot-in-the-door" technique, a sales tactic that aims to convince someone to make a major purchase or behavioral change by requesting a series of small concessions rather than a complete commitment all at once. The Ben Franklin effect, however, uses favor requests rather than concessions to achieve the same desired effect.

In Ben Franklin's autobiography, he outlines this strategy—an insight he identified way back in the 1700s. After being unanimously elected clerk of the General Assembly in Philadelphia in 1736, he won reelection the following year, but only after an affluent and influential Assembly newcomer made a long speech in support of Ben's opponent. Ben was a bit of a pistol and recognized he needed to nip this in the bud, as he sensed this newcomer's influence would only grow with time, so I'll let him tell you what happened next in his own words:

> *I therefore did not like the opposition of this new member, who was a gentleman of fortune and education, with talents that were likely to give him, in time, great influence in the House, which, indeed, afterwards happened. I did not, however, aim at gaining his favour by paying any servile respect to him, but, after some time, took this other method. Having heard that he had in his library a certain very scarce and curious book, I wrote a note to him, expressing my desire of perusing that book, and requesting he would do me the favour of lending it to me for a few days. He sent it immediately, and I return'd it in about a week with another note, expressing strongly my sense of the favour. When we next met in the House, he spoke to me (which he had never done before), and with great civility; and he ever after manifested a readiness to serve me on all occasions, so that we became great friends, and our friendship continued to his death. This is another instance of the truth of an old maxim I had learned, which says, "He that has once done you a kindness will be more ready to do you another, than he whom you yourself have obliged."[1]*

Remarkably, Ben Franklin turned an adversary into an ally by asking him for a favor! This is backed up by a 1969 study in which participants were awarded prize money by a researcher based on their performance in an intellectual contest. Participants were then randomly split into three groups:

1. One-third of the group was approached by the researcher, who asked them to return the prize money, saying he had self-funded the study and was now running short.

2. One-third of the group was approached by a secretary, who asked them to return their prize money, saying it was from the psychology department, whose funds were now running short.

3. One-third of the group was not approached at all—this was the control group.

Each group was then surveyed about their feelings toward the researcher. Unsurprisingly, the group approached by the secretary to return the money liked the researcher less than the control group did. However, Group #1, the group the researcher approached himself to ask for the funds to be returned, liked him *more* than the control group did! A personal request for a favor in this case increased liking, whereas an impersonal request decreased it.[2]

Counterintuitively, allowing someone to do you a favor is an incredibly powerful way to gain her loyalty. If I were to go on vacation and ask you to mow my lawn while I was away, I would obviously be indebted to you. You did me a favor, and I "owe you one." What is less obvious is that—by "allowing" you to do me the favor of mowing my lawn—I've increased the likelihood that you will perform further (and greater) favors for me in the future.

It is this insight, first delineated hundreds of years ago, that the TIARA Framework builds upon. In an informational interview, you are asking someone for a small favor of time and information. By not returning this favor immediately (as Ben Franklin pointedly refrained from doing), you increase the amount your contact likes you, as well as the likelihood he will help you again in the future!

As humans, we are capable of rationalizing incredible behaviors (both positive and negative) to prevent cognitive dissonance—the uncomfortable feeling of holding conflicting feelings or opinions simultaneously. Eventually, a sense of causation forms in our brains, so we retroactively justify our previous favors as having been done *because* we liked that person or group of people.

Therefore, when you check back in with someone with whom you've previously had a good informational interview, she'll be tempted to help you simply to justify her previous investments of time and effort in you. The informational interview should therefore be viewed as both a short- *and* a long-term investment.

Maximizing the benefit of an informational interview in the long run is the subject of the next chapter. We have more pressing matters to attend to right now, however—specifically, conducting a good informational interview. That starts with *good small talk*—the first phase of our three-phase TIARA Framework.

Phase 1: Small Talk

Is good small talk something that can be created? Or is it more a matter of luck?

I hope you know by now that I don't really believe in luck! I *almost* believe in "creating your own luck," but that's still too *Dirty Harry* for my tastes. Instead, I believe in maximizing the probability of desired outcomes.

Ultimately, nothing in the job search is guaranteed, but having the right plan in place in advance gives you the highest chance of success. The probability of creating good small talk is no different. Small talk comes very naturally to some people, and not so much to others. I'm definitely in the latter category. Therefore, during my own previous job searches, I had to find ways to make it systematic. It's far more possible than you might think.

So how do I maximize my chance of creating good small talk?

In short, take a genuine interest in the other person. Furthermore, give the person a chance to talk about whatever he or she wants to talk about—especially initially. The first rule of facilitating a good conversation is "follow the energy," so if your contact becomes more energetic in response to a question, stay with it for a follow-up question or two. If not, just move on to the next one. The questions I would open with are the following:

1. "How is your day going so far?" The answer gives me a sense for my contact's demeanor—chatty or all business? This also gives me potential content for follow-up questions that demonstrate I am actively listening, such as if the contact mentions car trouble or a current project.

2. "What projects are you working on right now?" This demonstrates that I have an interest in the type of work the contact actually does, plus it allows me a chance to gauge the person's passion for his or her work.

3. "Can you tell me about your background and how you came to work for your employer?" In effect, I am asking the "Tell me about yourself" question before the contact can ask me. This again gives me a sense for how personal or professional the contact prefers to be. Does the contact mention hobbies, or is it all work-based? Manners also dictate that this question will be reflected back, which is why it's important to have prepared your answer to "Tell me about yourself" in advance!

During the small-talk phase of the conversation, you will spend your time mirroring the topics and demeanor of your contact. In this phase your primary goal is to build rapport (you may also gain usable information here, but that is less critical). So speak about hobbies if your interviewer does, and avoid them otherwise.

Similarly, if your contact takes only thirty seconds to answer your question about his or her background, you should spend only thirty seconds describing yours. On the other hand, consider two minutes the maximum for any single answer you give to any question the contact presents to you. Therefore, if he or she takes five minutes to answer that question, you still only take two minutes before moving on to the Q&A portion of the conversation.

What if my contact and I find we're from the same hometown, support the same sports team, or so on, and she wants to continue talking about that?

By all means, do so! You're forming rapport, which is the primary goal of this conversation! The usable information can always be collected later, but rapport (which usually precedes advocacy) has to happen initially or it is unlikely to occur.

For example, one job seeker I worked with was competing with another candidate for an attorney position. She was told later that she had received the offer in part because she had asked a partner about a picture of her dogs on her desk during the small-talk phase of the interview, and they struck upon a common passion for rescue dogs. The partner effectively told her later, "You can *trust* someone who loves rescue dogs."

Whether it's bonding over rescue dogs, being raised in a large family, or the Chicago Cubs' awful odds of winning the World Series yet again this year, *follow the energy*.

This algorithm for small talk is not foolproof, but it gives those of us to whom small talk does not come naturally a structure for systematically attempting to break the ice and establish rapport!

How long should I stay in the small-talk phase before moving on to Q&A?

Although there is no exact answer to this question, given that your main strategy is to follow the energy shown by the interviewer, I would say expect the small-talk phase of the conversation to last about five minutes. You can bridge this transition with a comment like, "Thank you again for your time. I did prepare some questions for you, so I'm hoping I could ask you those now." The questioning algorithm that follows is where the TIARA Framework gets its name.

Phase 2: Questions and Answers

I've never known what questions to ask during informational interviews, but is a "questioning algorithm" really necessary?

Necessary? No. Incredibly helpful? Yes, especially if you've never known what to ask before. Knowing what questions to ask and the preferred order will dramatically improve your ability to turn informationals into job interviews. Furthermore, *knowing* you know that information will greatly reduce your anxiety about this step of the process.

Can't I just be direct and ask them, "Can you help me find a job?"

No, unfortunately. Although this approach would be efficient for you, it scares away potential advocates who won't feel comfortable giving you any meaningful help until you've earned their trust and fondness.

The questioning algorithm you'll learn in this chapter, called TIARA, will guide you through the Q&A portion of the informational interview to help you do exactly that—earn your potential advocate's trust and fondness—thus maximizing your chance of converting this informational into an actual job interview.

Why is it called TIARA?

TIARA is simply an acronym for the five topics you'll cover during the Q&A phase of the informational: Trends, Insights, Advice, Resources, and Assignments. This structure maximizes the likelihood of having a successful informational interview that both builds rapport and provides usable information.

Another benefit of the TIARA acronym is that it's easy to remember on short notice, because occasionally informationals can occur without any warning whatsoever! Have you ever been seated at a table of strangers at a conference luncheon or wedding reception, where making conversation is pretty much required? All of these situations are potential informational interviews. TIARA will actually help you negotiate these situations as well.

The "small talk" described earlier as Phase 1 of the TIARA Framework applies only to informational interviews; it doesn't work elsewhere as small talk. However, TIARA actually *does* break the ice when "making conversation" is required. Furthermore, because these people are strangers, they're perfect candidates to practice your technique on because you have nothing to lose. (I myself default to TIARA in such situations, simply out of habit and because I like how it gets people talking in a meaningful way.)

Consider TIARA to be the CPR of informational interviewing— a replicable, reliable routine. TIARA guides you through the process of earning a person's trust and fondness, enabling you to conduct an informational on a moment's notice (even without research, when necessary).

The fundamental thesis of TIARA is that you'll begin the conversation by treating your contact as an expert. Over the course of the informational, your questions will shift in tone and depth so you frame your contact more personally as a mentor, maximizing the chance that you'll turn this stranger into an advocate. So without further ado, here is TIARA:

- **T**rends

- **I**nsights

- **A**dvice

- **R**esources

- **A**ssignments

Before I go into each step of TIARA, let's do a quick thought experiment. Put yourself in the position of the contact. Imagine you are at work and you get a call from someone (let's assume it's a fellow attendee of your undergraduate university), and after some small talk as outlined earlier, his first question to you is, "What do you recommend I do to get a job with your employer?"

How far do you think you might go beyond trite and obvious answers like "Keep networking"? You don't really know this person very well, so exposing your personal network to him without knowing him better seems awfully risky. After all, it would reflect poorly on you if you passed him on to a colleague, and he was similarly awkward and forward in *that* conversation, too (a fair assumption). Plus, you are not thinking particularly creatively at this point in the conversation—you are still probably thinking logically about the deadlines and emails you've put on hold to take this job seeker's call.

In short, the job seeker's request is too abrupt. He's made only a cursory attempt to get to know you, so you in turn are likely to make only a cursory attempt to *help* him. Something is missing here between small talk and a request for advice. This job seeker is attempting to turn you into his mentor without first acknowledging your expertise.

Simply saying "I acknowledge your expertise" won't cut it, either. This job seeker needs to give you a chance to show off some of that expertise before asking for your mentorship. You could be completely clueless or a total maniac for all he knows! Just as you wouldn't trust someone offering to buy your car sight unseen, you certainly wouldn't trust a job seeker who asks for your advice without kicking your tires first! The best way to probe your expertise is with some open-ended yet engaging questions about your professional experience. This increases both trust and likability.

Small talk—Phase 1 of the TIARA Framework that we discussed a moment ago—gives you a systematic way to warm your contact up before asking anything of him or her. Using the TIARA questioning algorithm in Phase 2 (Q&A) ensures that any requests you *do* make are nonthreatening and aligned with your previously declared focus on gathering information and insight—not asking for a job. Your contact, if treated properly, may *offer* you assistance with helping you find a job, but that is her prerogative and shouldn't be requested (at least not in this conversation, anyway).

So what sorts of questions should I ask during each step of TIARA?

Remember that we don't want to "stump the contact," nor do we want to spend a lot of time digging up research-based questions that may be seen as transparent attempts to impress (an approach that Ben Franklin would surely frown on!). The ideal questions for TIARA are ones that allow the contact to talk about whatever he wants to talk about. These are open-ended questions that engage the contact creatively, and they're generic enough to be durable over multiple conversations (although they will inevitably become more sophisticated over time). Here's another look at TIARA, with a sample question from each step of the interview, to give you an idea of where we're headed. Then we'll look at each section in more detail.

Trends: "What trends are most impacting your business right now?"

Insights: "What surprises you most about your job?"

Advice: "What can I do right now to best prepare for a career in this field?"

Resources: "What resources should I be sure to look into next?"

Assignments: "Which projects are most common/important in your work?"

TREND QUESTIONS

Trend questions are an excellent way to open an informational interview, because whether your contact is a junior or senior employee of his firm, he will readily be able to provide interesting answers that allow him to feel smart. The only difference will be the scope of business that his insights cover. Some good trend questions are:

- "What trends are most impacting your business right now?"
- "How has your business changed most since you started?"
- "How do you think your business will change most dramatically in the next several years?"

These questions require no research, they make your contact think in a *real* way, and you can ask these questions of five different employees and receive five different answers. The versatility, depth, and durability of these questions make them extremely effective openers. A chief information officer may discuss very macro technology trends impacting her business in an informational, whereas a second-year programmer may instead discuss one particular trend in much greater detail, reflecting the shorter scope of his experience to date—however, both perspectives are extremely helpful. Plus, these are the type of questions that are likely to make your contact say, "Give me a second to think about that . . . ," which indicates she is truly giving you an original and accurate answer that reflects the best of her expertise and experience, rather than trite, easy advice requiring no thought.

Besides, it's much more fun as an interview subject to discuss what trends you think are most impacting your business than it is to describe the corporate culture. People enjoy talking about themselves more than they enjoy talking about their employers. Granted, all of these questions are asked *in the context* of your contact's current employer, but they all focus on getting the contact to really try to give you the best information she can. We want the person to truly engage, and these questions are a great way to do that.

Won't that sort of question seem overly simplistic to an informational interviewer?

Not unless you have an informational interview subject who enjoys answering technical questions more than personal ones! In fact, these questions' simplicity is what makes them great options for those of you who are new to informational interviewing.

However, recognize that your versions of these questions will become more sophisticated over time. For example, let's say I do an informational with a marketing manager at Kraft on a Monday, and I ask, "What trends, in your opinion, are most impacting your business right now?" In reply, my contact says that rising oil prices have compelled them to overhaul their distribution strategy to minimize fuel costs, which they fear could skyrocket at any moment.

Next, during my informational with General Mills on Wednesday of that same week, instead of asking simply, "What trends are most impacting your business right now?" I can ask the same question in a more credible fashion—for example, "During my research I've learned that rising oil prices are causing consumer packaged goods companies to radically redesign their distribution strategies to reduce shipping costs. Are you seeing a similar trend, or are other trends having a greater impact on your business right now?"

This is essentially the same question: "What factors are most impacting your business right now?" The only difference is that I demonstrate some knowledge in the second iteration with the General Mills contact, showing him I've done my homework prior to that conversation. This industry insight encourages the contact to give me an even more sophisticated answer, which I can then use to improve future iterations of the question in subsequent informational interviews. It's a virtuous cycle—good information begets further good information.

Remember that the goal here is to keep the contact's energy level high. If she clearly enjoys this line of questioning, stay with it. Ask follow-up questions to her answers; for example, "What is involved in redesigning a distribution strategy, particularly for someone in marketing?"

You may get to ask only one question before the conversation takes off, or you may get a chance to ask several Trend questions, but once the energy seems to level off, that is your signal to move to the next step in TIARA, Insights.

INSIGHT QUESTIONS

Insight questions are very similar to Trend questions, but they start to become slightly more personal, rather than strictly business-related. We want the contact to gradually become more comfortable disclosing personal information to us, and that starts with getting him to share his personal feelings. Here are some good Insight questions:

- "What surprises you most about your job/your employer?"
- "What's the best lesson you've learned on the job?"
- "What's been your most valuable experience at your employer so far, and why?"
- "If you had to attribute your success at your employer to one skill or trait, what would it be?" (This is especially effective for more senior or recently promoted contacts, with a good follow-up being "Is that trait shared by many across the firm, or is it unique and you've adapted it to your advantage?")

Again, these questions do not require research, yet they build rapport with your contact—simply because they are fun to answer.

Your contact is *the* world's foremost expert on her own insights, so they can't be wrong. These questions also require your contact to activate the creative part of her brain (this will be essential later), and they allow you to demonstrate a genuine interest in her experiences and insights. Furthermore, the information you collect here can be incredibly useful, meeting our secondary goal in the informational interview process!

How can the answers I get from Insight questions be useful later?

There are many ways, but the most significant way is that it opens your contact up to further personal disclosure (and ideally empathy) later in the interview, because you've demonstrated a genuine interest in what the contact has to say. In addition, you've kept your word that this conversation would be about the contact's experiences and insights—not a job. The later steps of TIARA require a high level of trust to be effective, so it's important to take your time during the initial steps.

These answers are also useful during future interviews, both informationals and job interviews. As we learned in the last chapter, the ability to source information is incredibly powerful for establishing credibility—instead of making a sweeping generalization about this employer's work-hard, play-hard culture with no tangible proof, being able to attribute that assertion to current Product Manager Catherine Kelly dramatically sets you apart from other candidates. You are a safer pick to advance than one who (1) is less networked at the firm, and (2) makes assertions without hard proof during informationals.

Similarly, being able to source your assertions is useful in any formal cover letters you may be asked to prepare. The term "cover letter" tends to refer specifically to the 250- to 350-word letters summarizing interest and qualifications for a specific position—this is the occasion when this sourceable information is especially helpful, because it's critical that in the first paragraph you establish the reasons for your interest in the firm and identify for the hiring manager who your key advocate there is.

Finally, answers to Insight questions are also useful in that they allow you to form a mosaic of the industry, function, and employer you are attempting to join. Particularly for those of you who are attempting to change careers, this may save you from a significant career misstep. For example, many MBAs seek to become strategy consultants. This career involves constantly bringing structure to chaos, so being comfortable with ambiguity and incomplete information is an important prerequisite. Thus, if you hate ambiguity, strategy consulting is a poor career choice.

Career changers will hear different answers every time they ask a particular question from the Insight family, but over time the answers will converge to form very accurate patterns. I know this from my own experience. When I left my strategy consulting and marketing careers to enter career services, at first I had great misgivings. Would I miss the travel- and project-based nature of consulting? Would I miss the in-store visibility of my marketing work? After several informational interviews with my future colleagues, it became clear that what they enjoyed most about their jobs very closely synced up with what I had enjoyed most about my previous careers—the fast pace, the closeness to consumers, the ability to invoke dramatic change quickly, and the chance to improve my clients' quality of life.

Having this knowledge in my back pocket, complete with sources to back it all up, made me a much more confident and credible candidate; it allowed me to win my job at Duke over a candidate with a much more traditional career counseling background, so this stuff really does work. Again, follow the energy. When it starts to flag, or when you reach the two-thirds mark in your interview, you'll want to move on to the next step of TIARA, Advice.

ADVICE QUESTIONS

By now we've developed some rapport with our contacts and have engaged the creative parts of their brain in the conversation, so this is the time where we start trying to reframe our contacts as mentors rather than simply as experts. Mentors take a long-term interest in the welfare of their mentees, whereas experts may feel their work is "done" once they've imparted their wisdom to you. The onus is on the job seeker to convert the expert into a mentor, because advocates' benefits are not usually imparted immediately, and the Advice phase of TIARA is the best time to attempt this conversion.

Advice questions are actually very similar to Insight questions, except they involve one additional element the Insight questions did not—empathy. In this part of the conversation, we are actively trying to get our contacts to put themselves in our shoes, convincing them to give us not just vague advice for what we should do next, but the *actual* steps they would take if they were in our position *right now*. Good examples of Advice questions include:

- "What can I be doing right now to prepare myself for a career in this field?"
- "If I got hired, what should I be sure to do within the first thirty days to ensure I get off to the fastest start possible?"
- "What do you know now that you wish you'd known when you were my age or in my position?"
- "If you were me, what would you be doing right now to maximize your chance of breaking into this industry or function?"

Again, these questions are durable—they can be used over and over without becoming stale, and they do not require extensive research. The biggest mistake job seekers make in the informational interview process is thinking that the conversation is about themselves, when it is really about the contact. The TIARA Framework provides a structure that effectively makes this common mistake impossible, because your contact—not you—will be speaking for the vast majority of the interview time.

The ideal outcome of an informational is that your contact begins to view your job search success (or lack thereof) as a reflection *of her own ability* to give good guidance and/or be a good mentor.

If she actually gives you the best advice she can come up with, and you execute it all flawlessly (which you will, following the 2-Hour Job Search process) but still do not find success, you can go back to her with an update on your progress. This update will recap the advice she gave you, how you've followed it, and what results you've achieved; finally, *it will solicit further recommendations*.

I've heard stories from my students about certain Boosters becoming the job search equivalent of Robocop within their organizations at this point, following up with hiring managers they (the Boosters) contacted previously to get updates and asking additional coworkers whether they are looking for any solid candidates. Why is this?

Simply put, *nobody* likes to think they give bad advice or are terrible mentors—this, after all, causes cognitive dissonance, and people will go to great lengths to restore their belief that they are fantastic. In fact, this follow-up request for further recommendations kicks the Ben Franklin effect back in, wherein they like you even more in retrospect in order to justify their previous efforts to help you. Without gaining their empathy for your situation, this is impossible. The best advocates to have are Boosters who become your mentors through an informational interview, but your Boosters will need to give you thoughtful advice before they develop any sense that you are now a mentee of theirs.

It is essential to take excellent notes during this part of the conversation, by the way, and by hand—not by computer! Taking notes on your computer will likely be audible to interviewers, making them wonder whether you are truly listening or are just surfing the Internet or answering email while they are speaking. It will also force you to summarize your notes immediately after the conversation when they are freshest in your mind (this includes scheduling follow-up reminders, much as you do in the 3B7 Routine—we'll cover this in more detail in the next chapter). These notes will be *the* featured element of your first follow-up email following your informational (differentiated from your immediate thank-you note following the conversation), because they are what will trigger the Ben Franklin effect in the future.

Once the Advice section of the conversation has run its course, or when you are within a few minutes of the end of your scheduled time allotment, it is time to move to the fourth segment of TIARA, Resources, which includes the single most important question of the entire interview—one that I call "the pivot."

RESOURCES QUESTIONS

We've just finished asking our contact a series of questions designed to make him empathize with our situation, so he now better comprehends the challenges of finding employment in a market where "being qualified" alone simply isn't enough.

Resource questions are designed to elicit where your contacts go when they need or want information about their industry, function, or business. These can be people, places, or things. Obviously, we are most interested in people (namely, hiring managers to whom our contact will advocate for us), but we are bound by a promise we made when we reached out to our contact in the first place—that the conversation would be about his or her experience and insight, not jobs. Now, if the contact offers to *make* the conversation about jobs . . . but we'll get to that in a minute. It all starts with the *pivot question*:

- "What resources should I be sure to look into next?"

  and alternatively:

- "What next steps would you recommend for someone in my situation?"

Regardless of how long Trends, Insights, and Advice questions occupy your informational interview, it is essential that you make it to the pivot question before the conversation ends. This question is what allows you to determine how to wrap up the conversation. Thus, the pivot is always asked first before any other Resource questions.

Resource questions are designed to determine what sources of potential advantage your contact would leverage if she were in your situation. This ideally involves specific people—referrals. However, we will pursue these very gently. There are other Resources questions available to you, but we'll explore those later, after we see how our contact responds to the pivot question.

The pivot question is *purposely* vague about the sort of help you're seeking. We can't gracefully ask for handoffs to hiring managers, given that we said this conversation was about information and not jobs, but we can give interviewers a chance to gracefully *offer* those handoffs to us, if they are so inclined.

This question is called the pivot because—depending on your interviewer's answer to it—your conversation will go in one of two different directions. If he offers you contacts without your asking (expect this to be the exception rather than the norm—that way you're never disappointed), then you've hit the jackpot—you've found a Booster ready and willing to help you move your candidacy along. However, if the contact doesn't offer you such contacts right away (or asks for more specificity about the sort of help you're seeking), then the process of gaining advocacy from this contact will be more involved. In other words, your contact's response to the pivot question dictates the strategies you employ for the rest of the interview.

What if my contact offers to connect me to a hiring manager?

This is the jackpot scenario—your contact turns out to be a rabid Booster willing to open her network to you right away.

In response to the pivot question, she considers who the next person you should speak to at her employer should be, and either offers to connect you personally (for example, "Let me introduce you to Wendy—if you're a State alum and want to work for our firm, you'll have to go through her!") or gives you that person's contact information and grants you permission to use her name as a referral (such as "Here's Wendy's contact info, and let her know that you and I spoke").

Either referral method will suffice for your purposes, but you *must* obligate yourself to follow up with your contact in a couple of weeks to let her know how things turn out. *This is absolutely critical.* Set a reminder (à la the 3B7 Routine) for yourself two weeks from the day of that informational so it stays on your radar without your having to think about it.

Earlier I mentioned that one of the quickest ways to alienate Boosters is by not responding quickly (within a business day) when they offer you times for informational interviews. Equally destructive is not following up with a Booster after he agrees to help you, leaving your status a complete mystery to him after he put his reputation on the line for you with no personal incentive whatsoever.

This is bad manners, but even worse, it allows you no graceful course of action should the contact's contact not respond (and this happens fairly frequently). My job seekers who fail to obligate themselves to follow up often find themselves in an uncomfortable situation where they get no response, yet have no clear path forward for what to do next. This usually results in a weak request several weeks later, asking if the previous informational interview contact could follow up with the suggested referral contact to try to get that person to respond to you. This request appears needy, and given how easily you can avoid having to make it, there is simply no excuse for putting yourself in such a stressful and exposed position.

By telling a Booster who just offered you a contact something along the lines of, "Thank you so much! I'll reach out to Wendy immediately, and I'll check back in with you in a couple of weeks to let you know what happens," you have your bases covered. If you and Wendy connect and have a great conversation, you can let your Booster know this is the case and give her the satisfaction of knowing she helped someone in need. However, if Wendy never responds to your outreach, now you have no choice but to update your Booster about the situation, because you swore you would, and keeping your word at all times throughout this process is a must.

This update doesn't have to be negative, though. Your check-in phone call (remember, avoid email when things stop going smoothly with a possible employer) would simply be something like this:

Hi, Anna. This is Steve. Thanks again for taking the time out a couple of weeks ago to speak to me—that information was very helpful! Per your suggestion, I reached out to Wendy, and

I promised you I'd give you an update in a couple of weeks to let you know what happened.

Unfortunately, I haven't managed to make contact with her yet. Please let me know if you have any suggestions for how I can best proceed from here, and thanks again for your support. I truly appreciate it!

Note that if you get your Booster's voice mail, mention *only* the content from the first paragraph in your message, along with a request for a callback. Save the rest of it for an actual conversation.

A message like this carries several benefits. First, it shows your Booster that you are organized enough to not let "to-do" items fall through the cracks—you do what you say you will do. Second, it gives you a second chance at your Booster's contact with minimal awkwardness—after all, you're just keeping a promise to a Booster, rather than complaining about anyone else's shortcomings. Third, it allows your Booster to improvise next steps on your behalf.

Boosters will usually be willing to do more for you than you yourself would ask, so it is better to defer to their expertise for how to proceed if Wendy is unavailable, rather than ask them for a specific action—like to check in with her on your behalf. The latter is a closed-ended response, so the contact may follow up with Wendy—who, for example, may be totally overwhelmed by work or out of the office on sabbatical or maternity leave, so such a check-in may not do any good. It's better to ask your Booster what she'd recommend for you next—she may then recall that Wendy is consumed with launching a new product critical to the firm's success right now, and she will try directing you to a new contact instead.

In short, Boosters know best. Defer to their judgment whenever things start going wrong. This shows that you take direction well, know when to defer to experts, and will protect their brand by not "going rogue" when things don't go according to plan.

One quick note before we leave the jackpot scenario—if a Booster writes the email introduction for you and copies you on the message, reply to all to express your interest in speaking to that new contact soon. This way, the new contact knows the next move is clearly up to him. In fact, offer in your email to call at a certain time or suggest some times that are good to speak, if that would be most convenient for him. This confirms for your Booster that you've done your part. That said, I would shortly thereafter write the Booster a thank-you email (*without* copying the new contact) for making that connection, again with a promise to follow up with your Booster in a couple of weeks to report on what happened.

So that's the easy scenario. In short, if an informational interviewer appears to be a Booster and gives you a contact right away, follow these steps:

1. Thank the Booster.

2. Obligate yourself to follow up in a couple of weeks with the Booster to let her know what happened.

3. Initiate outreach to that contact immediately (or reply-all to the email your Booster sends introducing you to your contact).

4. Set a reminder for two weeks to follow up with the Booster, regardless of whether you have connected with the new contact.

It's not complex, but having a process for handling it makes it especially easy to manage. With any time remaining in the conversation, you can continue with the Resources questions we'll discuss in a moment in the "non-jackpot" scenario, because there still may be great potential for learning in this conversation.

So what do I do in the "non-jackpot scenario," when my interviewer asks me specifically what kind of resources I'm looking for?

You deflect the conversation toward nonhuman resources. The worst-case scenario at this point in the conversation is explicitly asking, "Who should I talk to next at your firm?" This implicitly violates your contention that you were interested in insights and advice rather than a job. Worse than that, however, is if your interviewer says, "Nobody

comes to mind right now, but I'll let you know if I think of anyone."
Ouch. Informational interview dead end. This behavior is fairly typical of Obligates, but Boosters may respond similarly when put on
the spot so directly.

Recall that I myself am an Obligate. I used to be a Booster, but
I was burned one too many times advocating for people who either
didn't follow through or followed through so poorly that it reflected
poorly on me. As an Obligate, I would never give a contact to a
stranger without checking that it was OK with my contact first. The
awkwardness of having to tell an informational interviewer, "Let
me check with my contact to see if it's OK if I hand you off to him,"
was so overpowering, I usually said, "Nobody comes to mind right
now," just to avoid such an uncomfortable moment. That way, if I
decide to hand him off and get my contact's OK later (which I'm
unlikely to do, given that I'll have myriad other distractions going
on), he'll be pleasantly surprised.

Boosters may *want* to offer you a contact but feel similarly pro-
tective of their network, given that they've known those people far
longer than they've known you. If your contact doesn't offer you
a referral contact immediately, don't ask for one—this gives you a
second chance to ask for one later. Executing that second-chance
request appropriately may even help you extract benefit from an
Obligate like me (leveraging the Ben Franklin effect), but we'll discuss how best to accomplish this at the end of this chapter when I
discuss Phase 3: Next Steps.

So how do I respond if an interviewer asks me for
clarification about what resources I'm seeking?

You'll deflect the questions away from contact seeking and toward
information seeking. Some examples of good Resources questions are:

- "What resources—for example, websites, blogs, or magazines—
  do you read regularly to keep current on your industry?"

- "What's the most important ten minutes of research you do
  each day to stay on top of trends impacting your business?"

- "If I wanted to learn the language of the industry—for example, common acronyms and industry-specific terminology—prior to actually entering it, what resources do you think might prove most helpful?"

These questions are far less threatening and are much lower risk than asking for contacts, particularly if you sense apprehension on the part of your contact. These questions are also durable—they can be used again and again, earning unique answers each time. Thus, although you are not getting contacts, you are still collecting usable information that will help you in your future conversations.

Remember, these Resources questions can be cut for time after you've asked the pivot question (along with a deflecting Resources question like one from the preceding list, if necessary). However, if time permits, move on to the final step of TIARA, Assignments.

ASSIGNMENT QUESTIONS

We have framed our contact as an expert and systematically converted a former stranger into a mentor over the course of our thirty-minute conversation. Assignment questions are purely focused on gaining usable information rather than building rapport. Their goal is to help you speak the vernacular of the industry, gain an understanding of the high-value work under way right now, and develop an answer to the question "We're not sure how we could use someone of your qualifications—what sort of work would you be able to do for us?"

This question is asked more frequently than you might think, especially at smaller organizations (remember that employers with two to ninety-nine employees account for two-thirds of all U.S. employment [see page 17]). These smaller firms may not have a vacant position waiting for you, but if you can explain how the employer could improve their bottom line by bringing you on, they may create a brand-new role for you.

Larger employers will usually know where a job seeker with your skill profile might fit in, but regardless of the employer's size, it is incumbent on you to be able to offer the organizations you approach some ideas about where you might fit in.

Here are some good Assignment questions:

- "What project (or projects) have you done for your employer that you felt added the most value?"
- "Have any projects increased in popularity recently at your organization?"
- "Have you had interns or contractors in the past? If so, what sort of projects have they done?"

The answers you get will help you build your mental toolbox of the types of projects that are increasingly in demand and importance at your targeted employers. When a potential employer says, "We've never hired anyone with your qualifications before—what sort of work could you do for us?" you should *not* respond, "I'll do anything you need me to." This demonstrates desperation rather than savvy, and it may result in you fetching coffee rather than doing any meaningful work.

Instead, invoke the "power of the first draft." It's much easier to critique someone else's ideas than it is to create them from scratch, so relieve your potential employer of that burden by instead suggesting roles for yourself and engaging the employer in why or why not such a role may be feasible. This increases their likelihood of coming up with alternatives, which are far easier to brainstorm than entirely new ideas.

To invoke the power of the first draft, suggest to the employer some projects that you would be capable of that you think may create value for them, based on what you've learned from your other informationals. In my earlier example, I could take what I learned from my Kraft and General Mills interviews to a smaller consumer packaged goods company. When they say they aren't sure where an MBA would fit into their company, it's far better for me to be specific and say, "I know fluctuating oil prices are driving your competitors to revamp their distribution strategies, so I could analyze your current structure to look for savings opportunities. I could also do a customer segmentation analysis or a market size estimation for your next new product under launch consideration, or I could manage a series of packaging redesigns you have under way." All of these projects may be ones the company already has in process or completed, but they demonstrate that I have an understanding of what my targeted position actually entails. This in turn makes me a much more credible candidate than one who says, "I'll do whatever you need me to do" to a firm that has no idea how to use an MBA in the first place!

Assignment questions can be cut for time, if necessary, but they give you a nice jolt of legitimacy right at the end of the conversation—before you enter Phase 3: Next Steps—because you're taking an active interest in the projects you'd likely be assigned if hired.

Should my questions change at all if the person I'm speaking to is much younger than me or has less experience?

Your questions will not change significantly—you will still spend the first half of the conversation framing the person as an expert and gradually converting him into a mentor. It is especially flattering when a more senior person expresses an interest in a younger one's insight, and these contacts will have viewpoints both of their immediate sector and of their firm in particular that are unknown to you.

It may feel odd to ask a junior graphic designer about the trends she is witnessing in her work when you may end up becoming her boss (or boss's boss) eventually, but her perspective will help you better understand the challenges the company is facing and an appreciation for what is happening in the trenches as well as at the 500-foot level. Is the employer keeping up with the new technology? Do the junior team members juggle multiple projects at once or handle one at a time sequentially?

So, no, the Trends and Insights sections will largely stay the same in this situation. The Advice section will change slightly in tone, but you can account for this by asking your questions from the junior employee's perspective; for example, "What best practices have you seen among the managers you've had at the firm?" This both gives you a wider perspective of the company and builds a Booster in the process.

The Resources and Assignments sections will also not change significantly when speaking with a younger employee. The critical step is getting your contacts to empathize enough with you to be willing to advocate for you in their organization—this comes from trust rather than knowledge, so take the time to treat them as the experts they are in their respective spaces. For all you know, it could be the first time in years that someone's asked this person's opinion—and as Ben Franklin learned, recognition of a person's uniqueness is sometimes all it takes to create a lifelong ally.

That said, with Q&A complete, it's time to move on to our finale, Next Steps.

Phase 3: Next Steps

So how do I wrap up this conversation? Especially given that my goal is to get an interview?

Well, if we hit the jackpot and found a Booster who immediately volunteered to pass us on to a relevant colleague, we already know our next steps—we will follow up with the referral we got from our contact, and update the Booster in a couple of weeks on our progress (or lack thereof). We simply state that aloud and thank the Booster for spending time with us, then send a quick thank-you email the next day.

If we don't get a referral immediately from our informational interview—and you should expect this to be the norm rather than the exception—you'll want to use what I call a Two-Part Informational Closing. This technique gives you a second chance to obtain referrals later, with a higher probability of success than if you put your contact on the spot and directly ask for referrals at this point. A Two-Part Informational Closing sounds something like this:

> *Our time is up, but thank you so much for your time today—you've given me a lot to think about, and it sounds like you're working for a great organization.*
>
> *I'm going to take a few days to process all of the information you've shared. If, on reflection, it seems like your organization and I may make a good mutual fit, is it OK if I reach back out to you to get your recommendations for how best to proceed from here?*

It would be very difficult for even the most obdurate of Obligates to say "no" to a conditional request like this one. *If* this seems like a good mutual fit, is it OK if *I* reach back out to you? This requires no effort from your contact whatsoever—the next steps are entirely on you—yet it is a very powerful illustration of the traditional "foot-in-the-door" technique, whereby gaining an initial small commitment increases the chance of getting a larger commitment later.

In psychologist Robert Cialdini's 1984 book *Influence: The Psychology of Persuasion*, he illustrates the power of getting a seemingly minimal and meaningless "yes" from a stranger, using a concept he calls "commitment and consistency." In one study he cites, an experimenter goes to a beach, lays a blanket five feet away from another beachgoer (chosen at random), and settles in with a cooler and radio for some quality time in the sun. Shortly thereafter, the experimenter steps away to grab refreshments or go for a short walk.

A few minutes later, a second experimenter happens by and pretends to steal the first experimenter's radio. The experiment measured the bystander beachgoer's response to the "crime."

Depressingly, in only 20 percent of cases did the beachgoer intervene, yelling, "Stop, thief!" or attempting to track down the stolen goods. However, one simple change was introduced into the experiment that dramatically increased the intervention rate from 20 to 95 percent—care to take a guess what it was?

When I ask for guesses from the groups I lecture to on this process, the answers range from "pay the beachgoer to watch his stuff" to "hide the radio with his blanket" to "turn the radio off before stepping away." In truth, all it takes to turn the detached bystander into a beach blanket vigilante is for the first experimenter to ask the test subject, "Would you mind watching my things?" before stepping away.[3]

Good manners make it nearly impossible to say "no" to small-probability requests like that one—turning that request down would usually require an elaborate story about an old war and/or football injury or the bystander's admission of her own imminent departure, as in, "I would, but I'm leaving in a few minutes myself." Barring that, though, an incredible 75 percent of test subjects (from 20 percent up to 95 percent) intervened *only* because they had verbally committed to watching the experimenter's things. The subject thus established (if only accidentally) a self-image as "someone who watches other people's things when asked," and the desire for consistency with that self-image and the desire to minimize the incongruence (or cognitive dissonance) inherent in breaking that promise compelled the subject to action.

That is how you get Obligates who agree to give you an informational interview to help you. You leverage their fear of awkwardness and bad manners to get them to make a tiny initial commitment, even if they don't really want to. Once they do that, they have further obligated themselves to be available in the future if you decide this is something you want to pursue (which it usually will be—it's a top target, after all!). To have their bases covered in case you do follow up, Obligates will likely do just enough legwork to give you *something* of value. This may simply be a few job postings they found internally, or some good websites to check in the future, but in some cases it's just easier for them to pass you on to a friendlier colleague or the actual hiring manager than to come up with a cover story for why they had to renege on their promise to help you.

Boosters likely won't need any formal psychological technique in order to be motivated to help you, but you'll probably need to use some with Obligates. Obligates can actually become very productive contacts through your proper execution of the "commitment and consistency" concept—eventually their self-image will grow to include "I'm the type of person who lives up to my commitments to assist job seekers I've promised to help."

Go into every informational interview assuming it's going to be a two-part informational—with follow-up required to get a useful contact. If you ask for a contact during an initial informational and fail to get one, you've hit a dead end with that contact—it's awful to lose a Booster simply because you put the person on the spot.

By ending the conversation with the Two-Part Informational Closing just described, you're allowing several positive developments the chance to occur offline. First, this delay gives your contact a breather during which she can decide whether she likes and trusts you enough to pass on to a colleague. Second, it demonstrates that the promise you made in your email was sincere—the entirety of your conversation *was* about gathering insight and advice, and not about getting a job. (That said, you've specifically prepared the contact to expect that your next outreach could be more explicitly focused on employment.) Third, it allows your contact a chance to touch base with their referral to see whether that person is available and willing to speak with you.

Finally, and most important, this technique once again allows you to maintain control of the follow-up process, just as you did with your 5-Point Email. Using the Two-Part Informational Closing, you are keeping your foot in the door so you have a second (and better) chance to get a referral from your contact a few days from now, even if the contact wasn't ready to offer one when you first spoke.

How do I conduct Part 2 of the Two-Part Informational Closing, then?

First, be sure to send a thank-you note for the initial informational interview the day after the conversation—this goes for informationals in which you got a contact as well as for those in which you didn't. Again, this is just good form.

However, when you know a Part 2 will be necessary, set yourself a reminder for the following business week (meaning a weekend has passed in between) to follow up with your contact—again, the reminder allows you to forget about the conversation until it is time to act, minimizing your stress.

If the contact has given you any advice that you can implement immediately—like starting to read *Brand Week* or *Ad Age* if you want to get familiar with marketing terminology—then certainly do so. Mentioning such immediate incorporation of advice in Part 2 increases your credibility by demonstrating you're the type who follows the advice you're given, which in turn increases your contact's willingness to invest in your welfare.

Now, to actually *execute* Part 2 of the Two-Part Informational Closing, when your reminder pops up, call your contact and simply say what you would have written in a follow-up email—something like:

> *Hi, Anna. This is Steve. On further reflection, I think your organization and I might be a great mutual fit. Per your offer last week, may I take a few more minutes of your time to ask you what next steps you'd recommend for me to maximize my chances of getting an interview with [the employer]?*

This conversation should take only a few minutes, and your contact may even choose to screen your call and help you over email instead. If you do get your contact live, and he gives you general Obligate-type advice like, "Keep doing what you're doing," ask the contact directly whether he can recommend anyone else for you to speak to in order to continue building your network at that organization. At that point, you have nothing left to lose! Not all contacts are created equal, unfortunately, but you might be surprised at how even Obligates will come through for you from time to time when they take that first step toward committing to help you.

If you *do* get a further contact during this follow-up session, thank the contact for his time and guidance, and, just like in the "jackpot scenario," promise to update him in a couple of weeks with the results of his assistance to you. If you don't get a contact or any helpful information from this follow-up, this contact is likely a dead end, indicating that you've hooked an Obligate at your target organization when what you really needed was a Booster. Thus, you'll start up the 3B7 Routine with a brand-new contact until you're confident you've found someone who truly wants to see you succeed.

Not every informational interview will yield results—that is why it is especially important to have a process whereby you prioritize your target employers (your LAMP list) before initiating a process (the 3B7 Routine) for systematically requesting, scheduling, and conducting informationals with your highest priority targets, simultaneously. When you job seek in this fashion, no single fruitless informational interview is a failure—it's simply an investment that hasn't paid off yet. As my dear mother used to say, "The difference between a bad meal and a good meal is about an hour"—that is to say, you might be a great fit, but simply are in the right place at the wrong time. Thus, in the next chapter, we'll discuss how to maximize our follow-up to achieve the best possible results from the informationals we do conduct.

TROUBLESHOOTING

What if my contact starts our conversation by saying, "I'm very busy and only have a few minutes to talk, so just tell me how I can help you"?

This happens somewhat regularly, unfortunately. The problem is that you have no idea whether the person truly is a Booster who suddenly became busy but still really wants to help or an Obligate who wants this to be over with as soon as possible!

Therefore, offer to postpone the conversation until the contact has more time. If the person gratefully accepts (and you two can agree on a date within the next week or so to speak before you hang up) you've likely found a Booster. You've also demonstrated excellent emotional intelligence by how you handled the situation, putting the contact's needs before yours. The contact now "owes you one," and you are continuing to build your track record of fulfilling your commitments and taking stress out of the contact's life.

If your contact resists rescheduling the conversation, that's a trickier situation. Obligates will be very resistant to postponing, because it's implied the conversation will be longer later than it would be now, and their "obligation" will hang over them even longer than it already has. That said, Boosters do also respond this way, recognizing that speed trumps time if they are Super-Boosters who simply want to get you connected to the right people as quickly as possible.

In either case, if the contact insists on having the conversation right then, I'd advise you to immediately jump to the Advice section of TIARA (but with a dash of Insight thrown in) with a question like, "Given what you've learned in your time at your employer, what would *you* do, if you were me, to maximize your chance of getting an interview?" You are requesting insight, empathy, and creativity all at once—it's the one-question version of TIARA, basically.

continued

TROUBLESHOOTING

How your contact responds to this will be telling. If she resists engagement, speaking generally and in the second-person with a response like, "Just keep talking to people here, and eventually you'll find an opening," you've probably found yourself an Obligate, the job search equivalent of landing a giant rubber boot while out fishing. Hey, it happens. It's a cost of doing business, and not every raffle ticket will be a winner.

However, if the contact speaks more specifically and in the first person—for example, "If I were you, I would reach out to Tim Daggett and ask him for his perspective—I know he's looking for some people right now, and I can introduce the two of you via email if you'd like . . ."—it's likely you've found a busy Booster who genuinely wants to help but simply needs to do so quickly, given his other commitments.

If the earlier question isn't your style, you can skip the integration of Insight and go straight for the job search jugular with a pure Advice question. I suggest asking, "What do you know now that you wish you knew when you were in my position as a job seeker?" The nature of the response will still fall into either the Booster or the Obligate camp. If the person resists giving you any real advice, you've found an Obligate and need to keep following the 3B7 Routine to find a Booster. However, if you do get a real lead, then assume the person is a Booster and pursue that recommended avenue as if you had conducted a full-length informational with the Booster; that is, obligating yourself to follow up in a couple of weeks with the results of the proffered help.

However, if the referral does not respond and your Booster doesn't offer to assist you further (or respond at all) when you report your lack of results, the presumed Booster was probably just an Obligate seeking to "pass the buck" to a colleague. Again, no worries—it's part of the process.

In general, when a contact tries to rush through an informational interview it's a bad sign—most likely you've found an Obligate. That said, this strategy will help you find the occasional Booster needle in the Obligate haystack.

What if my contact cancels our conversation at the last minute and then becomes difficult to reschedule with?

Try to reschedule the conversation to the best of your ability, but recognize that this is *very* typical Obligate behavior. She's hoping if she treats you poorly enough you'll go away. Très junior high, but such is life. Simply grant the Obligate's wish and move on; keep following 3B7 until you find someone who's genuinely interested in your welfare.

What if a contact agrees to speak with me, but warns me in advance that his employer is not hiring right now?

TAKE THAT CALL! If the person was an Obligate, he'd do whatever he could to avoid actually scheduling this conversation with you. However, if the person is happy and excited to talk to you anyway, you may have found a Super-Booster.

Informationals with firms that aren't hiring are great for several reasons. First, there's no pressure. Second, if you leave a good impression, you're at the top of the contact's list when the employer does start hiring again, because you demonstrated a genuine interest even when told jobs were off the table. Third, and most important, Boosters at a nonhiring firm have the potential to help you with multiple firms rather than just their own!

Remember Adam's story from the List chapter? An IT consultant who wanted to get into the mobile phone industry, he found a job with the mobile industry's standards board because he conducted informationals with employers who told him in advance they couldn't hire him. Adam used

continued

those conversations to build his knowledge of the industry and the credibility of his interest, and when it came time for the pivot question in TIARA, he had license to directly ask his interviewer, "What other organizations should I make sure I have on my radar right now, given my job search goals?" and "Which firms in this space are doing exciting things right now?"

His Booster couldn't help him with his own employer, but he could give him contacts at several less-obvious smaller organizations that, thanks to their lower profiles, weren't being inundated by interested candidates.

Boosters *want* to help you. When their own employers are not an option, Boosters are liberated to connect you to employers elsewhere (and you are similarly liberated to *ask* about other employers), which can lead to connections at several firms instead of just one. Instead of treating this situation as a dead end, treat it as a risk-free chance to find out which organizations are on the rise.

What if a hiring manager tells me I'm simply not a fit for her firm?

Most employers would not be so direct. They'll prefer more ambiguous language like, "We'll keep your application in our database, and we'll reach out to you if we identify a potential fit." A rose by any other name smells as sweet; in this case, sadly, "We'll keep you in our database" still usually means "no."

Regardless, this is why we have a LAMP list. When we have a Booster who gives us a specific timeline (for example, "Check back in with me in mid-April—that's when we start identifying projects"), set yourself a reminder to reconnect with that employer then. After that, move on to the next new employer on your LAMP list. Conversely, when an employer tells you employment is not an option—for whatever reason— simply open your LAMP list, delete the employer, and send your first outreach email to the next target on your list. No thinking, just execution.

TROUBLESHOOTING

Rejection stings momentarily, as it should—this is what compels you to reevaluate your previous efforts and seek feedback. That's growth—an ability universally appreciated by employers. It's also a call to action. You have too many other targets to be wasting time on one who has bad taste in potential employees . . .

## CHAPTER 10

FOLLOW-UP

So I just conducted an informational interview—now what?

The benefits of informational interviewing rarely reveal themselves immediately. The goal of this chapter is to help you extract the maximum benefit from each Booster you do identify in a systematic and efficient fashion.

Many job seekers who are new to job searching, away from the confines of a school's recruiting office, expect informational interviewing to be like fishing for fish. You bait the hook, toss the line in the water, a fish swims up and grabs it, and there's your dinner.

Unfortunately, it's actually a lot more like fishing for lobster. Lobsters are a little slower, a little more cautious, and thus they don't respond well to baited hooks. Instead, you need to set baited-cage traps for them in the ocean, which you check back on every few days to see whether any were caught. That is the most maddening aspect of the job search—there is *zero* instant gratification.

My students face a major challenge with this arrangement—not only because engaging in social activities provides immediate rewards, but also because even *schoolwork* provides a more predictable reward than the job search does. You spend an extra hour studying for a statistics test, you gain more confidence immediately and receive a proportionately better grade later. In contrast, if you spend thirty minutes conducting an informational interview, it can take weeks or even months before you know whether that effort results in an interview—let alone a job.

Because the job search offers such uncertainty and long-delayed rewards, committing to a structured approach is critical—otherwise, it becomes far too easy to avoid or abandon a job search before your efforts have a chance to yield positive returns. Most students consider finding a good job the primary reason for going to school in the first place, and most unhappily employed graduates consider a better job to be the fastest route to a happier life. If you've read this far, you're obviously interested in committing to such a structured approach, but recognize that a systematic follow-up process is just as important as a systematic outreach process.

So how do I systemize my follow-up?

Anytime you have *any* informational interview, send a thank-you email the next day. (Emails reach your contact faster and are easier to archive than hard-copy thank-you notes.) This person did you a favor, so regardless of the outcome, she's earned your thanks.

In addition, if the contact offered you a contact referral immediately, you've obligated yourself (in your thank-you note if not in the conversation itself) to provide an update on your progress in a couple of weeks.

Beyond that, you will want to set up a recurring one-month reminder in your outreach calendar after each informational interview. Your Boosters may not know how to help you at the moment of your first conversation, but if you've left a good impression, they will start hearing things about potential job openings that they had previously ignored.

Even Boosters will filter out information about job openings unless they have a candidate in mind. Once you give them a reason to care, however, they become an extra set of ears for you. If you check back in monthly, you'll accomplish several goals—you'll remind them you're still seeking, you'll renew your interest in their firm specifically, and you'll give them a prompt to take action (because clicking Reply for whatever reason seems infinitely easier than clicking New Email or Forward).

What should these monthly check-in emails consist of, exactly?

These check-in emails start off simple and get even simpler over time. They also—like everything else in this process—follow a pretty basic pattern. The first check-in in particular is quite formulaic, yet very effective.

A month after any informational interview (good or bad) that did not result in a referral, your first calendar reminder should pop up to check back in with your informational interview contact. (Recall that if your informational *did* result in a referral, you'd have already updated your original contact with your progress a couple of weeks ago.) The basic structure of this check-in will be as follows:

1. Thanks again

2. Recap of advice given in previous conversation

3. Summary of benefits derived from following that advice

4. Request for further suggestions

In practice, a check-in email could look like this:

SUBJECT: Progress update

Dear Anthony,

Thank you for again for speaking with me last month. I found your insights incredibly helpful, particularly on the increasing importance of microsegmentation in the advertising space.

Also, per your advice, I started reading *Brand Week* and *Ad Age* to get a better sense for current trends in marketing and advertising. I'm now feeling much more able to converse knowledgably about the challenges and opportunities facing ad agencies these days.

Do you have any additional suggestions or recommendations that you think may prove helpful? Any further guidance would be greatly appreciated, but if nothing comes to mind, I'll be sure to keep you posted on my progress over the coming weeks.

Best regards,

James

The first update email will be the longest one, as you have to refer to your notes from your prior conversation, reiterate any advice they may have given you, and describe your follow-through. If you receive additional advice in response to this outreach, repeat the process—incorporate their advice, note how you benefit, and save the results for your next check-in. If you receive no response, simply wait until the following month's reminder to follow up.

The second follow-up email will be much shorter, looking more like this:

Second, third, and later follow-ups will get shorter, usually consisting only of a continued appreciation of their help, a reminder that you are still actively looking, and a request for any additional advice they may have.

These monthly check-ins may not seem like much—again, they are rather formulaic. However, they are the equivalent of periodically checking your lobster traps for a catch. You are providing your Boosters with a service—a reminder to act if they've heard anything that might be relevant to you. Remember, Boosters *want* to help you, and even Obligates may forward you an internal posting if you make it easy enough (meaning you make it so easy that they simply *can't* justify not helping!).

Will these follow-ups become burdensome as I work my way down my LAMP list?

As your network of advocates at your target employers grows, you will indeed spend more and more time checking back in and following up with your Boosters. But these follow-ups can always be done by email, and their format really won't change much after the first one. It truly is more the thought (or more specifically, the reminder) that counts. The time that each follow-up takes will be minimal— you'll simply just be doing it more often.

In the meantime, once you feel you've identified a quality Booster at a top target on your LAMP list, continue initiating outreach to the next employer down on your list. The process doesn't get more complicated or harder as you go along—you simply repeat Step 2 (Contact) and Step 3 (Recruit) until you land an offer. It's repetitive, but not difficult.

Using the 2-Hour Job Search, your probability of success grows with each new relationship formed and Booster identified. Eventually, your network will grow so wide that you'll be offered job interviews with relative regularity, due to the ever-growing advocacy network you've created.

Lest you think this process is an infinite loop, rest assured that in practice none of my job seekers who've adopted this process has gotten much further than number ten or number fifteen on his or her LAMP list before something panned out.

It wasn't just their adopting a systematic approach to the job search that got them hired, though. With that systematic approach came a newfound confidence, one that was visible in their interviews. They knew there were dozens of other fish in the sea, and recruiters always have and always will find candidates who project such confidence more desirable than others. Organizations want employees who create plans of action for their projects, replete with contingencies for when things go wrong. Candidates who clearly have other lines in the water are more likely to be that kind of employee. (According to the 80-20 Rule, at any rate . . .)

TROUBLESHOOTING

What if I follow up with a person I thought was a Booster, and he doesn't respond?

Don't take it personally! Again, some people, when they don't have anything to say, may simply say nothing at all. The periodic prompt is simply a gesture of gratitude on your part for your Boosters' help, and keeping them updated on your progress even when they offer nothing in return further demonstrates the genuine, sustained nature of your interest and your organizational ability to keep them looped in to what you are working on.

The job search is a game you win only once (per job)—therefore, *most* of the outreach you conduct won't lead to job offers, just as you won't buy *most* of the houses your realtor shows you. There's simply no way to know which particular conversation, contact, or email will yield that all-important job interview. So you keep having lots of conversations, developing new contacts, and sending out new emails to improve your chances of landing that lucky winner. Going in knowing that success will be the exception rather than the rule should help you slog through the slower times.

Step 3 Wrap-Up

There are a number of different outcomes for each informational interview, but they fall more or less into one of three different categories: **Advance**, **Hold**, and **Drop**. Advances are where your contact (either immediately or after a scheduled follow-up) connects you directly to a hiring manager or asks you to send her a resume that she can pass along herself. This is the ideal outcome, and if the job is indeed available, the Advance usually leads to an interview in a matter of weeks. As always, you'll promise to update your contact with the results of her Advance in a couple of weeks, so you can use that update as a way to check your status for that particular opening.

It's a Hold when a contact still responds to your follow-up outreach but doesn't have any further helpful information at the current moment. It is the empty lobster cage—no catches today, but that doesn't mean it won't have dinner inside waiting for you tomorrow. You're effectively in a holding pattern with these contacts, so focus your efforts elsewhere until it's time to check in with them again.

It's a Drop when a contact stops responding to your follow-up inquiries. This is why I like to include in my follow-up emails at least one question, either personal or professional (for example, "How did that product launch project turn out for you?" or "How is little Billy doing?")—something that prompts your contact to give you a brief, simple response. That response shows that your contact is still actively engaging with you—increasing the chance that he is likely still keeping an ear out for job opportunities you may find relevant. If there is radio silence after a couple of check-ins, however, you should start trying to find a new contact—a repeated lack of response points to a disengaging Obligate rather than a committed Booster.

Employers are trying to compress the amounts of time they spend on hiring—it isn't productive (in that it won't immediately improve an employer's bottom line), so the process now moves faster than it ever has before. This plays to your advantage if you follow the 2-Hour Job Search, because employers will start with the applicants they know before reviewing any strangers' resumes. It bears

continued

repeating: employers today vastly prefer finding "good enough" candidates quickly rather than "perfect" candidates slowly!

"Good enough" candidates are usually found through personal connections and internal referrals—very rarely are they found by their resumes alone. Therefore, the general rule of thumb I suggest is to *never* send a resume to anyone unless it has been asked for. An unsolicited resume is unlikely to be read, and makes you look desperate.

With this approach, when your resume *does* get asked for, you know it is likely to get reviewed and/or forwarded, giving you information you didn't have before about that contact's willingness to help you and the employer's potential interest in your candidacy. An employer won't hire you without seeing your resume, but just because you send your resume doesn't mean it will be seen!

The follow-up process doesn't fundamentally change even if the contact does ask for your resume—you'll still offer to check back in two weeks to provide an update. However, you'll *also* keep repeating the process with other targets in parallel—outreach, informational, follow-up—until a job offer is made. Initially this process may seem scary, but you'll get used to it. Eventually, it will become as routine as brushing your teeth or watching your favorite movie for the hundredth time, but unlike those activities, each new iteration of the 2-Hour Job Search offers the potential to *fundamentally* change your life for the better!

CONCLUSION

It's counterintuitive, but right now is a great time to be looking for a job. The advent of online job postings fundamentally changed how hiring gets done. People flocked to the concept due to its convenience and logic. However, in practice online job postings have proven to be nothing more than a massive red herring.

Submitting resumes online lets job seekers feel like they're looking for a job, so job seekers continue to use them, knowing full well how unlikely a response is. It's like watching someone beating up a vending machine for an hour, completely unwilling to accept that it just ate his or her money. Unfortunately, whoever invented the online job posting didn't invent a way to screen out unqualified or mediocre candidates.

The 2-Hour Job Search doesn't offer the same instant gratification that filling out online job postings does—it involves change, and its rewards (while far larger) are slower to arrive. Unlike online job postings, however, it *does* work.

What makes right now such a great time to be looking is that, using the 2-Hour Job Search (either wholesale or cafeteria-style for the parts you struggle with most), you are being strategic while others are flailing.

Dick Fosbury wasn't necessarily the best high jumper in the world in 1968. He actually struggled at the sport in high school, finding himself unable to use the traditional "straddle method" due to a back deformity. Out of desperation, he resorted to an out-of-fashion technique called the upright scissors method. He found he *was* coordinated enough to do that—at least good enough to make his high school track team.

However, from this basic technique, he found his results improved as he leaned back during his jumps. Gradually, he modified this style even further so that he started going over the bar backward, head-first, and face-up—thus, the "Fosbury Flop" was born.

He was the only person at the 1968 Olympics to use that method, and he won the gold medal, breaking the world record in the process. In the next Olympics in 1972, twenty-eight out of forty of the high jumpers had adopted the Fosbury Flop technique, and today pretty much every elite high jumper uses it.[1]

He cleared the highest bar that day in Mexico City, but Dick Fosbury may *not* have been the best high jumper in the world—just the best equipped. He had simply evolved beyond the rest of the field—his new "technology" (even with his limited coordination) trumped his competitors' superior natural abilities.

It's frustrating to know that jobs don't go to the most qualified candidates these days, just as it must have been infuriating for Dick Fosbury's opponents to experience defeat at the hands of such an unorthodox approach. However, the job search has never been fair. Are resumes mailed in on nice paper really a fairer way to select whom to interview than choosing only from a pool of internal referrals? Viewing the job search through the lens of "fairness" can drive you mad. It simply is what it is.

By reading this book, you have learned a process by which you can exploit the "new rules" of the job search. These rules are not a fad, either—even if the economy reached new heights tomorrow, there would still be no going back to the pre-Internet job search days.

Technology—specifically, the online job posting—has broken the traditional job search. Luckily, it broke the job search *for everyone*—in that sense, it's actually a more "fair" time to find a job now than ever before. The job search is experiencing its own Gold Rush era, in which those who figure out how to find and collect the gold first get rich, while the rest struggle to survive.

Jobs today are going to those who adapt most quickly and effectively to those new job search rules, and my goal in writing *The 2-Hour Job Search* was to tell you *exactly* how to do that. The great news is that you can have a less impressive resume than other candidates but still get a job with the right strategy. David *can* slay Goliath, but not without a slingshot.

On the flip side, remember that if you get complacent, you too can get Fosbury Flopped over by inferior candidates who implement this method before you do. Superior qualifications used to "speak for themselves," but the world is far too noisy for that now. If you've long been a Goliath in your industry, and you've suddenly found yourself in the job search, let this book help you reboot your career.

With this book, I wanted to demonstrate that the job search—while tedious—is utterly accomplishable. Even so, some of you may now be looking back and thinking this change in approach seems insurmountable. Perhaps you're not comfortable with spreadsheets, or informational interviewing still seems too socially awkward to even attempt. Please resist that urge. Everyone is bad at an activity before he or she is good at it (do you remember your first piano or violin lessons? If not, I'm sure your parents do . . .), and the job search is no different.

In her 2006 book *Mindset*, Stanford psychology professor Carol Dweck identified a concept called the "growth mindset" that is particularly relevant to the still-skeptical among you. Fixed-mindset individuals tend to think that talents are largely static and strongly tied to one's natural abilities, while those with growth mindsets think that talents are like muscles—they can be developed over time with practice and effort, just as muscles can be stretched and microscopically torn so they grow stronger than before.

Interestingly, those with growth mindsets have been shown to adapt to change more effectively, cope better with failure, and even progress further in their careers. Even more interesting, *the growth mindset can be learned!*

The beauty of the 2-Hour Job Search is that it is largely repetitive once the basics are established. After the first few 3B7 Routine iterations and informational interviews, you'll be mastering these techniques the way a twelve-year-old masters a new video game a week after his birthday.

I've watched the ambiguity and hopelessness of the job search bring adults to tears and rip families apart. It's truly awful. I hope this book has shown you it doesn't have to be that way. The job search will *always* be tedious and frustrating at times, sure, but it should never be overwhelming.

There's another helpful concept I'd like to highlight from Chip and Dan Heath's fine book *Switch*, mentioned in chapter 2. The authors stress that "shrinking the change"—or viewing large problems as a series of smaller tasks—is critical to adopting a totally new approach to solving a task. In this book, we've shrunk the change by turning the job search into three discrete steps: Prioritize, Contact, and Recruit.

In Step 1: Prioritize, we learned how to build a list of forty possible employers in forty minutes, using four different methods requiring just ten minutes apiece. We then collected three pieces of data that approximated the likelihood of success for each one. This gave us two resources: a large universe of possibilities and a precise order in which to pursue them, all in just over an hour.

In Step 2: Contact, we learned that less is more. Shorter outreach emails—particularly the kind created using the 5-Point Email process—are not only easier and faster to write, but they also maximize the probability of getting a response from Boosters (that is, the *right* kind of contacts) while helping to screen out Obligates and Curmudgeons. We also learned an airtight tracking system in the 3B7 Routine, so that we could strategically ignore any to-dos that didn't require action on a particular day, leaving us more mental bandwidth to focus on time-sensitive tasks each day.

Finally, in Step 3: Recruit, we learned a process for managing informational interviews to maximize the chances of meeting our dual goals: building rapport and gaining usable information. We learned which kinds of research were most critical to do in advance, how to initiate small talk, and how to systematically lead the conversation to earn that contact's advocacy. We finally learned how to follow up with those advocates systematically so minimal thought would be required, but potentially great benefit could be extracted.

Even shrinking the change doesn't make job searching *fun*, but it should improve your quality of life. I hope that, at a minimum, reading this book has removed most of the guesswork and confusion from the job search for you. You will still no doubt experience setbacks and curveballs along the way. I've tried to prepare you for the most common ones, but the new ones you encounter (which I hope you will share with me!) represent the insight portion of this process. That's where innovation happens, and when the 2-Hour Job Search becomes your own.

QUICK-START GUIDE

This guide is not a substitute for reading the rest of the book. However, it should refresh your memory enough to help you execute the steps we covered earlier, saving you from having to flip back and forth between steps.

Here's what we learned:

STEP 1: PRIORITIZE (THE LAMP METHOD)

1) List column (40 minutes total—4 approaches x 10 minutes per)

   a) Dream employer approach (see page 25)

      i) Type any "dream employers" that come to mind into the L column of your spreadsheet.

      ii) Determine common traits shared by your dream employers, and log employers who similarly meet those criteria.

   b) Alumni approach

      i) Search alumni databases for organizations where alumni hold interesting job titles in interesting locations.

c) Posting approach

    i)   Search Indeed.com for organizations with currently available job postings of interest to you.

d) Trend-following approach

    i)   Google trends in industries or functions of interest (such as "marketing trends") for employer ideas.

2) Alumni column (10 minutes)

a) Search your most recent alumni database for alumni at each employer in the L column.

b) Note only Y for yes and N for no in the A column—do not copy contact information.

3) Motivation column (5 minutes)

a) Assign target employers in the L column a qualitative score of 1 to 5, assessing your motivation to approach each.

    i)   Award a score of 5 to targets you find most motivating ("dream employers").

    ii)   Award a score of 2 to targets you are familiar with but find least motivating.

    iii) Award a score of 1 to targets you are completely unfamiliar with.

4) Posting column (15 minutes)

a) Using Indeed.com, classify current hiring activity. A 1 to 3 scale should work in a majority of cases; for example:

    i)   Award a score of 3 for hits found when searching for "<employer name><job keyword>."

    ii)   Award a score of 2 for hits found when searching for "<employer name>" but not "<employee name><job keyword>."

iii) Award a score of 1 when no hits are found for either of above options.

b) The P column's scoring scale is highly customizable, so reread this chapter if you are uncertain which scale is most appropriate for your particular search.

STEP 1: WRAP-UP—SORT LAMP LIST IN THIS ORDER

1. Motivation (largest to smallest)

2. Posting (largest to smallest)

3. Alumni (reverse alphabetically, or Z to A)

Change targets' Motivation scores (as desired) based on job posting quality, alumni contacts, or additional research of unknown employers, and sort again.

Your final list should resemble the sample on page 75.

STEP 2: CONTACT (BOOSTERS, OBLIGATES, AND CURMUDGEONS)

5) Naturalize (20 minutes)

a) Identify top-priority employers (say, those in your Top 5) with Ns in the Alumni column.

i) If none, proceed to step 6.

ii) If one or more, use the following algorithm to convert Ns into Ys:

(1) Most recent alumni database (*already done*)

(2) Previous alumni databases

(3) LinkedIn (Group connection or first- or second-degree connection)

(4) Facebook

        (5) Fan Mail

        (6) Cold calls

    iii) Once a target is found, note source.

  b) Utilize emails4corporations.com as needed.

6) Email (20 minutes)

  a) Locate email address for most relevant contact at each of Top 5 target employers.

  b) Write 5-Point Email to each contact.

7) Track (10 minutes)

  a) Follow the 3B7 Routine for Top 5 target employers.

    i) Set two reminders in Outlook any time a 5-Point Email is sent to a new contact:

        (1) Reminder #1: three business days later

        (2) Reminder #2: seven business days later

    ii) If a response is received before Reminder #1 pops up, you likely have found a Booster—schedule an informational interview as soon as possible.

    iii) If no response is received before Reminder #1 appears, initiate outreach to a second contact using the 3B7 Routine.

    iv) If no response is received before Reminder #2 appears, follow up with the original contact.

  b) Initiate contact with new target employers beyond Top 5 whenever a Booster has been identified, an employer is ruled out, or time permits.

STEP 3: RECRUIT (INFORMATIONAL INTERVIEWING)

8) Research (15 minutes per interview)

    a) Conduct external research.

        i) See DataMonitor360 analysis (when available).

        ii) Review positive headlines on front page of target's website.

        iii) Google both interviewer and employer for any negative headlines.

    b) Prepare for the Big Three.

        i) "Tell me about yourself."

        ii) "Why are you interested in our company?"

        iii) "Why are you interested in our industry and/or function?"

9) Discuss (30 minutes per interview)

    a) The three phases of a TIARA Framework informational interview are:

        i) Small talk

        ii) Questions and answers (TIARA)

        iii) Next steps

    b) Small talk should occur naturally, but can be induced systematically if it does not.

        i) "How is your day going?"

        ii) "What are you working on?"

        iii) "What path did you follow to join your employer?"

    c) TIARA is the guide for Q&A:

    Trends

    Insights

Advice

Resources

Assignments

    d) During next steps:

       i) If a referral is offered, commit (and schedule) yourself to follow up in two weeks.

      ii) If a referral is not offered, transition to Two-Part Informational Closing.

10) Follow-up

    a) Set monthly reminders to update those with whom you've conducted informational interviews.

       i) First update email should recap advice given and benefits gained, ending with a request for additional suggestions.

      ii) Subsequent updates serve primarily to update contact on your progress and request any additional suggestions.

    b) Time spent "harvesting" Boosters will grow as progress is made, but should remain minimal compared to outreach to new targets on LAMP list.

    c) Repeat Steps 2 and 3 until contacts lead to interviews and employment!

ACKNOWLEDGMENTS

The one common perspective shared by the best job seekers I encounter is that the job search is about others, not themselves. You need the help of others to get opportunities, as well as the *support* of others to keep you sane en route. I myself would like to thank some people who gave me this opportunity and kept me sane en route:

- My family—I truly couldn't have done this without your support.

- My beautiful and brilliant girlfriend, Amanda—I can't thank you enough for standing by me through this process, patiently helping review my awful early drafts and making me laugh when I needed it most.

- My agent, Richard Morris—thank you for your months of steady insight and confidence in this book's potential.

- My editors, Sara Golski and Julie Bennett at Ten Speed Press— how you made this readable, I have no idea!

- Dan Heath—you were the first person who *never* doubted this project's potential, and your mentorship throughout has been invaluable.

- Peter DiCola, Tim Nangle, Jean Ro, Javier Izquierdo, and Melissa Gudell—for everything.

- Professor Dan Ariely—without your insight on social versus market norms, this book never would have gone beyond LAMP.

- My amazing Career Management Center colleagues at Fuqua, especially the coaching team: Mary Beck, Beverly, Meg, Lisa, Ed, Ryan, Catherine, Catie, and Sheryle.

- Sam Rhodes—without the help of this wonderful cartoonist, this project may never have happened. Thank you for all of the mock-ups that helped people see this book's potential.

- David Purvis—thank you for taking such a great picture on such short notice!

- Jessica Thomas—thank you for sharing you own book publishing experiences with me when I was just getting started.

- Mike Stracco—I've had many great teachers over the years, but I never would have developed my writing voice without your AP English class. Thank you.

- Beth Corcoran, Ankur Seth, Roger Austin, and Jeremy Schifeling—you each customized this process in an important way, so thank you for your collaboration.

- Veronica Ho and Ivan Kerbel at Yale's School of Management—thank you for your advocacy and belief in my material when I was getting underway.

- The city of Durham, NC, especially the Mad Hatter Bakeshop—thank you for the many coffees during my marathon Monday writing sessions.

Finally, thank you to all of you who've picked up this book and/or attended my lectures. *The 2-Hour Job Search* is truly a living process, and your feedback and suggestions are what allows it to evolve in tandem with the market. I hope this book has helped you find what you're looking for.

NOTES

INTRODUCTION

1. Roy F. Baumeister, Ellen Bratslavsky, Mark Muraven, and Dianne M. Tice, "Ego Depletion: Is the Active Self a Limited Resource?," *Journal of Personality and Social Psychology* 74, no. 5 (May 1998): 1252– 65.

2. www.eweek.com/c/a/Enterprise-Applications/Full-Text-of-1002-Ballmer-Memo/1.

CHAPTER 1

1. Edward Lowe Foundation, http://youreconomy.org/pages/states/us.lasso?region=comp&-session=YEplus:980396D61da43226F3RSh1DD5A6C.

CHAPTER 2

1. Douglas Brinkley, *Wheels for the World* (New York: Viking Adult, 2003).

2. *Encyclopedia Britannica Online*, s.v. "Henry Ford," accessed September 20, 2011, www.britannica.com/EBchecked/topic/213223/Henry-Ford.

3. David Hounshell, *From the American System to Mass Production,* 1800–1932 (Baltimore: The Johns Hopkins University Press, 1985).

CHAPTER 3

1. Dan Ariely's 2008 book *Predictably Irrational* explores the concept of arbitrary coherence very effectively.
2. www.apa.org/research/action/multitask.aspx.

CHAPTER 5

1. Mark S. Granovetter, "The Strength of Weak Ties," *American Journal of Sociology* 78, no. 6 (May 1973): 1360–80.

CHAPTER 9

1. Benjamin Franklin, *The Autobiography of Benjamin Franklin* (New York: Henry Holt Company, 1916).
2. Jecker, J., and D. Landy, "Liking a Person as Function of Doing Him a Favor," *Human Relations* 22 (1969): 371–78, http://changingminds .org/explanations/theories/ben_franklin_effect.htm.
3. Robert B. Cialdini, *Influence: The Psychology of Persuasion* (New York: HarperCollins, 1984).

CONCLUSION

1. Robert S. Welch, "The Fosbury Flop Is Still a Big Hit," *Sports Illustrated,* Sepatember 12, 1988, 22–25.
2. Chip and Dan Heath, *Switch* (New York: Random House, 2010).

ABOUT THE AUTHOR

STEVE DALTON is a senior career consultant and associate director at Duke University's Fuqua School of Business. He holds an MBA from the same institution. Prior to entering the career services industry, Steve was a twice-promoted strategy consultant with A. T. Kearney and an associate marketing manager at General Mills. He lives in Durham, North Carolina. Visit 2hourjobsearch.com.

INDEX

229

More Career Guidance from Ten Speed Press

Resume 101
A Student and Recent Grad Guide to
Crafting Resumes and Cover Letters
that Land Jobs
by Quentin J. Schultze
$12.99 paperback (Canada: $14.99)
ISBN: 978-1-60774-194-7
eBook ISBN: 978-1-60774-195-4

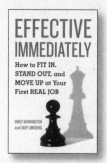

Effective Immediately
How to Fit In, Stand Out, and
Move Up at Your First Real Job
by Emily Bennington and Skip Lineberg
$14.99 paperback (Canada: $18.99)
ISBN: 978-1-58008-999-9
eBook ISBN: 978-1-58008-421-5

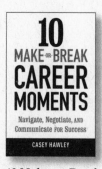

**10 Make-or-Break Career
Moments**
Navigate, Negotiate, and Communicate
for Success
by Casey Hawley
$13.99 paperback (Canada: $16.99)
ISBN: 978-1-58008-723-0
eBook ISBN: 978-1-58008-396-6

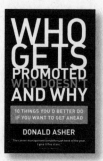

**Who Gets Promoted,
Who Doesn't, and Why**
10 Things You'd Better Do If
You Want to Get Ahead
by Donald Asher
$14.99 paperback (Canada: $18.99)
ISBN: 978-1-58008-820-6
eBook ISBN: 978-0-307-79769-8

Available from Ten Speed Press wherever books are sold.
www.tenspeed.com